My First
One
Hundred
Poems

ROBERT ERNEST RHINES

MY FIRST ONE HUNDRED POEMS

iUniverse books may be ordered through booksellers or by contacting:

iUniverse
1663 Liberty Drive
Bloomington, IN 47403
www.iuniverse.com
1-800-Authors (1-800-288-4677)

ISBN: 978-1-5320-4760-2 (sc)
ISBN: 978-1-5320-4761-9 (e)

Print information available on the last page.

iUniverse rev. date: 07/19/2018

Contents

52 year guy

52 two years, living a blind eye,-
Who am I, what kind of guy.-

Been places,-
Stared into the eyes of evil faces.-

From parking lot fights, to barroom brawls,-
Been there, done that, all.-

Collapsed lungs, from being stabbed with a knife,-
One inch longer, or a rib, boom out goes my life.-

Notice things, how they are, not as you see,-
A twist within me.-

I have lived.....
I have given.....
I have died.....
I have risen.....

Been thinking more and more lately,-
If women love me, and men hate me.-

Four knotches on my life, four times I've died,-
Some by accident, others I tried.-

Some thoughts, got me thinking,-
Free from drugs, of all kinds, and no drinking.-

I feel, I've been here, not just now,-
Just can't put my finger on it, I don't know how.-

To many deja vu,-
To many things, I know how to do.-
To many things, I still want to try,-
A bucket list, for a 52 year old guy.-

Diving from the sky, diving in the sea,-
Vacation in Australia, on a walk about, works for me.-

I can't do everything this time round,-
And I won't be lost, now that I am found.-

For you Father, of the land,-
Your return, is in high demand.-

We all sit and wait,-
Recollection, no set date.-

THE END

Written by: Author and Poet
Robert E Rhines
January 20, 2018
Copyright applies

1000 mile blind date

Tennessee to Texas, the longhorn State,-
On a 1000 mile blind date.-

Closer you get, heart races to its own beat,-
As the mile markers flyby, you lay back in your seat.-

Though we have lived in the same hometown,-
First formal meeting, live Friday as the sun sets down.-

On the walkway to the door,-
Meeting first time, of many more.-

Reaching out, ringing the bell,-
Door opens quickly, what the hell.-

Just a kidder you'll see,-
Try not to laugh to hard, your pants you'll pee.-

Hugs and kisses, let get something to eat,-
A pizza place right up the street.-

We giggle looking at each other, acting shy,-
A tear of joy, enters the eye.-

Laughter rolls, smiles are lit,-
A 1000 mile blind date, this is it.-

Eating a pie, conversation all the while,-
Definitely worth the wait, seeing your smile.-

The kiss, fingers in the hair,-
Ending the night, exchanges we share.-

After the night, morning we awake,-
Kisses first thing, the love we make.-

The timing was perfect, well worth more, than the wait,-
We pulled it off, on a 1000 mile blind date.-

THE END

Written by: Author and Poet
Robert E Rhines
December 6, 2017
Wheels rolling
~Expressing the Rooster~

Abused

Woman and children, everyday abused,-
No reason, no excuse.-

Called ugly, called a fool,-
Everyday verbally abused.-

Kept a prisoner, in your own home,-
He won't leave you alone.-

No where to go,-
Abused little, by little it begins to show.-

You want to tell someone, but who'll care,-
He slapped you around, and pulled your hair.-

Names are called,-
Your eyes have not just cried, but bawled.-

Hold it together, your the glue,-
Depend on yourself, your kids need you.-

Put down,-
Kicked around.-

He doesn't deserve you, he's mean,-
He's lowered your self worth, your self esteem.-

Black shades, to cover your eyes,-
To hide abuse, to hide your cries.-

Is there nothing to help with the pain,-
Will you ever be the same.-

Think about running, Its no use,-
So you stay, you take the abuse.-

Trauma in the long run, has set in,-
Damaged, but repairable my friend.-

He's torturing you still, from the grave,-
Don't let him win, now your safe.-

You have people that care,-
Being real, life isn't fare for all, not at all fare.-

We get damaged, we live with trauma,-
I pray for your kids, and you, there mama.-

Your loved, beyond belief,-
Your free now, he's gone, some relief.-

Take it easy, take it slow,-
You got this girl, I know.-

Dry those tears, from your eyes,-
Silence is broken, laughter cries.

Friends,-
Til the end.-

THE END

Written by: Author and Poet
Robert E Rhines
January 25, 2018
Copyright applies

Altering change

My life holds, many secrets,-
Skeletons in my closets are few, some regrets.-

But I've grown,-
My life is my own.-

Learning alot through the years,-
I've shared laughter, I've shared tears.-

Worst of times,-
Best of times.-

I see life for what it's worth,-
From skills I've acquired, to my children's birth.-

Relationships that come to an end,-
Life seems to stop, then begin.-

All the best keys we hold,-
Not paying attention when were young, but
understanding when were old.-

First part is caring,-
Never hold inside, what's worth sharing.-

Second part,-
Laughter is medicine for the heart.-

As is music, soup for the soul,-
Hearing other's words, learning as we go.-

For any friendship, trust and honesty,-
That part for happiness is key.-

Life's altering change, through choices I've made,-
Real friends stay, the rest will fade.-

Lock up the past, the future is yours, so live,-
With that said, these are the words I give.-

Low self esteem, set aside,-
Bury the past, laugh, love and enjoy, be companionate,
enjoy life.-

We can alter our own,-
Choices we make, at the end of the day, we both have
grown.-

THE END

Written by: Author and Poet
Robert E Rhines
January 15, 2018
Copyright applies

A man, just a man

Knock, knocking at your door,-
No, I am not God, no I'm not the Lord.-

A man, just a man,-
Bringing forth visions I've had.-

Luminous moon, glowing light,-
Casting the dense shadows, in the dead of night,-

But hence, the sun shining bright,-
Under the mask of the day light.-

Advocating mysteriously, under its silence,-
I bring forth a message, with reverence .-

A man, just a man,-
With visions, in my head, with dreams I've had.-

No powers I hold,-
But revelations of this day foretold.-

You think your walking alone,-
No where to go, no home.-

From the ashes we rise, from the dust of the earth we're
born,-
Everything living, to every loss we've mourned.-

A man, just a man,-
With dreams in my head, to these visions I've had.-

Three moons from this night,-
As the moon shines, under its mask of darkness, stars
as bright,-

Your not lost, your weaknesses broken,-
Read these words, hear these words I have spoken.-

I am the messenger, on hand,-
A man, just a man.-

THE END

Written by: Author and Poet
Robert E Rhines
February 11, 2018

Answers

Wandering aimlessly, this latter part of my life, somewhat confused, somewhat lost,-
Pull it together, gypsy in the wind, teach, your in control, your the boss.-

Endless thoughts no action, destination, question why am I here,-
Contiplating factors, mathematically, it doesn't add, subtract or multiply, it's like I am always bringing up the rear.-

Destiny set, pre destined for this I am not,-
With knowledge, I hold no special key, I'm not better, it's all I got.-

Thinking you may, I'm all but wealthy, far from wise,-
Though these set beneath my own eyes,-

Second breath I've forgotten, remember all, even one such as me,-
In store, out of stock the next chapter begins, can it really be.-

As I stand before you, all is bright,-
Shimmering reflections of me within you, from the sunlight.-

I must go when it's my time,-
Can you survive, what I've been through, before your
end, did you shine?-

I have asked not much of one,-
Not of a father, nor of a son.-

Not as a husband, has any other man?-
Do for you all that I can.-

As a soldier for Christ, this i know,-
I have forgiven all debts, your judgement is with him,
what you owe!!-

THE END

Written by: Author and Poet

Beyond Damaged

An ever innocent glo, warmth and the sweetest smile,-
Holding it true upon her face, beyond damaged all the while.-

Laughing, joking not seeing what's behind,-
Almost child like, not of age beyond damaged somewhat clever, nonetheless so unkind.-

She marvel's when the upper is hers, and will take,-
Wants to be clean from the outside, beyond damaged make no mistake.-

Her goal is pulling you unwilling, unaware into a taste of her one all you need,-
Like a boyish first crush you'll fall, beyond damaged now plants the seed.-

The wickedness and morso you'll feel her cold,-
A heart that's more beyond damaged than her story she told.-

All faults are on the hands of others,-
Noticed by none beyond damaged two sisters or mothers.-

Unwise to capture this heart,-
Manipulates, beyond damaged games start.-

Kind spirit she shows off at first glance,-
Becomes ruthless look close beyond damaged, no second chance.-

There's nothing you can get her heart to feel,-
Cold to the core beyond damaged, for real.-

Maybe somewhat pretty, soft on the eyes,-
Serious oh no, beyond damaged let's begin tell lies.-

Battle has more than begun,-
Over the top beyond damaged don't look back, just run.

THE END

WRITTEN BY: author and poet
R.E.RHINES
SEPT. 17,2017

Broken

Way, way back in the day,-
When your ancestors were made.-

Something amiss, something aloof,-
Something happened, something broken, an error in
your DNA, a goof.-

Ask me, how I am feeling? Do you want to know,-
A moment of conversing, now you gotta go.-

How to explain, what my mind is like, inside of me,-
Haunted in my dreams, broken from things, you
can't see.-

Ask me, how you holding up,-
Another round, and a shot of bourbon in my cup.-

You really care??
Carrying this burden, pieces, now broken, broken pieces
i won't share.-

Another moment, squirreling around in your chair, like
a kid,-
Broken inside, pieces put away, out of the way, hid.-

Lonely pieces, nor pieces, can you see,-
But I am broken, broken inside of me.-

No longer come here, don't come around,-
Holding back tears, quietly the words I'm choking down.-

Friends avoid me, because why.-
Because the pieces broken, broken inside.-

I'll be there for you,-
It's down to that, and it is not true.-

There on the streets, and turn away,-
Into pieces, I'm broken, broken before that day.-

My heart hammers bits and pieces, inside my chest,-
Broken, my soul finds no rest.-

I'm tired of pretending,-
Broken never, mending.-

I want this to all go away,-
Broken, let's fix this okay,-

Remember this, as you read,-
Broken, now your freed,-

THE END

Written by: Author and Poet
Robert E Rhines
January 29, 2018
Copyright applies

ullies

From the teachers, to the bleachers, all kids in between,-
Bullies are not tough, just plain mean.-

From the bus to the gym,-
And back again.-

Bullies put on a show,-
Until someone steps up, and says No.-

From the playground to the lunch line,-
Eating lunch and visiting, should be a fun time.-

Bullies step in, and cause a fuss,-
The jocks don't worry, what about the rest of us.-

From the locker room and in between class,-
We shouldn't have to watch our ass.-

Bullies are commonly rude,-
Put us inside the trash cans, or take out food.-

From the last class of the day,-
To the bus stop, in fear all the way.-

Bullies pick on the weak cause they can,-
They think it's funny, or makes them look like a man.-

From the ride on the bus,-
Why is this happening to us.-

Bullies beat us, and calls us names,-
Take our property, and play games.-

From walking down my driveway, thinking as I walk,-
These guys are never going to stop.-

Bullies are all bad,-
As individual's there sad.-

Mess with us, and in the end,-
We'll all have the last laugh on you friend.-

Leave us alone,-
If you can't, go home.-

THE END

Written by: Author and Poet
Robert E Rhines
January 25, 2018
Copyright applies

Busybody

Busybody, don't bother me,-
Just cause you got a master's degree.-

High fluting attitude,-
Middle finger in the air, how rude.-

Flash your money, flash your house and your cars,-
Fancy clothes, fancy drinks, fancy bars.-

Busybody, chosen words,-
Fussing up a storm, just to be heard.-

High dollar rings on your fingers,-
High dollar scents that linger.-

Flash your shoes, flash your phone,-
Fancy is you, now leave me alone.-

Busybody, let yourself be on your way,-
Mind your business, or have a bad day.-

High and mighty,-
Sticks and stones, alrighty.-

Run your mouth, run your tab,-
Drive yourself home, not calling a cab.-

Busybody, pull on over and stop,-
Couldn't stay between the lines, pulled over by a cop.-

Flash a badge, show a gun,-
Now what's the problem, son.-

Failed, field sobriety tests,-
Breathalyzers, next.-

Busybody, though yourself so cool,-
Delayed reaction for being a fool.-

DUI your done,-
Couldn't mind your own, into everyone else's fun.-

Busybody mind your own, I'll mind mine,-
And we'll get along just fine.-

THE END

Written by: Author and Poet
Robert E Rhines
January 25, 2018
Copyright applies

Choose wisely

I'm empty, been taken,-
My kindness for weakness, definitely mistaken.-

Many times misled,-
From words, your mouth has said.-

Out the door gone, I gotta go,-
Walking away, without saying no.-

To the arguments, the fights, I call a truce,-
Same ole, same ole what's the use??

It's up, it's down,-
A twisted roller coaster ride, all around.-

It's high, it's low,-
Mood swings come, mood swings go.-

It's not been nice, definitely crazy,-
Don't worry about me, I'll make it baby.-

We've had our time, time to run,-
We've had our laughs, we've had our fun.-

There's no need to swear, no need to fight,-
The beginning is over, the ends in sight.-

Soon after, the memories will fade,-
Like the love, we've made.-

Even though, we're now at the end,-
It's still fresh, those you chose over me, my friend.-

I have to stay solid, to the core,-
This chapter is over, I close the door.-

THE END

Written by: Author and Poet
Robert E Rhines
February 2, 2018
Copyright applies

Close those Eyes

Evidently it's not bad enough to be good, or good enough
to be bad,-
Sometimes were happy, sometimes were sad.-

Portraying story lines,-
Laid out, time after time.-

Take a second after you read, close those eyes,-
Go there in your minds.-
See the preface, the plot, the stories unwind,-

Behold,-
The stories told.-
Not all braising not always bold.-

But within the words written,-
Not being harsh, not being smitten -

It happens, it's life, it's all real,-
You laugh, you cry, no big deal.-

It's not just girls that cry,-
I do while writing them, and I am a guy.-

I'll read em two or three times,-
It's amazing how it unfolds, to a story line.-

Close those eyes,-
Go there in your minds.-

If you can't see, a story behind the scenes,-
Maybe your not one for this kind of poetry.-

Close those eyes,-
Go there in your minds.-

Visualize the story,-
Some funny, some sad, some are happy, and others gory -

Open your eyes, now you see,-
Some relate to you, some relate to me.-

THE END

Written by: Author and Poet
Robert E Rhines
February 14, 2018
Copyright applies

Countless

Countless stars, countless waves,-
Countless souls, need saved.-

Mountains high, across oceans wide,-
Countless souls, try to hide.-

Countries worldwide, foreign lands,-
Countless souls, out of hand.-

States in there own state of mind,-
Countless souls, dark and unkind.-

Cities and towns,-
Everywhere, all around.-
Countless souls, lost and found.-

Foreign places,- foreign faces,-
Countless souls, he embrace's.-

From the back alleys, to the deepest woods,-
Countless souls, some bad, some good.-

Countless souls, saved this day, saved this night,-
Amongst them lost no more, is yours, is mine.-

From countless souls of the dark, counted now in the light,-

Countless souls, we are winning, counting all the souls,
black and white .-

Countless souls, from what's within,-
Your soul is counted, not the color of your skin.-

There's only two colors of souls,
Black and white,- Bound in the darkness, or saved in
the light.

Countless souls, none in peace,-
Count you in, count you out of these.

Counted soul, your return,-
Countless souls, you will learn.-

There's only one way,-
Is your soul is saved.-

THE END

Written by: Author and Poet
Robert E Rhines
January 28, 2018

owboy

The horse I ride, not to fast,-
As I cannot outrun, the past.-

The gun belt I wear at my waist, two colts I drawl,-
As they clear the holsters, a little faster then all.-

Many a men laid upon the ground,-
Faster gun in the West, won't be found.-

I ride in the saddle, sitting high,-
Wide brim hat, clean shaven, who am I.-

A cowboy, gun slinger a man of the west,-
Drawl your pistol, and fall like the rest.-

For dual pistols, sit upon my hips,-
Trouble on the thoroughfare, main street passes my lips.-

One end of the street, stands a contender,-
My colts bark out two shots, another life ender.-

Average life, a gun fighter died young,-
Even for me, the fastest gun.-

Cowboy I was,-
No recollection or cares for the cause.-

Here I lay, tombstone at my head,-
Faster gun, now I'm dead.-

THE END

Written by: Author and Poet
Robert E Rhines
January 13, 2018

eep Within

Deep within, your strength is undeniable, big, set inside
your chest.-
Natural ingredients, shows your human, unlike some
of the rest.-

The trauma of life, dealt an undeserving hand,-
You cannot fold, hold out, others would fall, where you
stand.-

Deep within, the ember's of pain boil, your inner soul,-
Rebound your emotions, get back in control.-

The trauma of life, is winning one by one,-
You can not give up, there's work to be done.-

Deep within, where love still remains,-
Keep moving forward, for yourself, in all your kids
names.-

The trauma of life, has sent you the ultimate test,-
Don't be a quitter, give in give up, be better than the rest.-

Deep within, you got to let the pain go,-
Keep that fire burning, in your heart, let love show.-

The trauma of life, this battle is not lost,-
Think about all that it's cost.-

Deep within, be a winner,
and win...........

Written by; Author and Poet
Robert E Rhines
November 2017
Friends til the End

epression

Depression, number one killer in the world,-
Has killed more than any single massacre.-

Depression, worse than any gun,-
Kills you slowly, painfully no fun.-

Depression, locked deep down inside,-
No where to go, no where to hide.-

Depression, sets in its here for good,-
It strips away your life, even from childhood.-

Depression, is no joke, no fun, no smiles,-
Eating away at your insides for awhile.-

Depression, it comes it goes,-
One day your happy, the next day depression show's.-

Depression, most of us lose our will,-
Corrections, are more than in a pill.-

Depression, suicide is not the way to go,-
I've attempted three times unsuccessful I know.-

Depression, just wanting to feel free,-
Now I understand it's not a sickness, it's a disease.-

THE END

Written by; Author and Poet:
Robert E. Rhines
The Thanks giving of 2017

evastation

Since the beginning of time,-
Year after year right on down the line.-

Devastation comes, in some degree,-
At some time, it's happened to you, and it's happened
to me.-

Whether it was, natural, or mother nature, it's a loss of
life,-
Father, mother, family member, close friend, stranger,
husband or wife,-

Devastation has intervened or crossed your path,-
Does it add up, balance out or equal to, do the math.-

It's hard to get over, get around, or get past,-
What's going to happen, at the end of days, the world
eventually will crash.-

Devastation, will surround us, some will be consumed,
others will fight,-
Hold up, protect, survive all that is right.-

Lots will fall, to weak for any other, give up, give in,-
Strength will come in numbers, only way to survive,
only way to win.-

Devastation, knows no mercy, has no guilt, has no heart,-
Comes out of nowhere, doesn't sneak up, don't let you be prepared, why it's smart.-

Devastation, is horror, painful, and leaves it's victims traumatized,-
Quick, clean, in and out no prisoners no crimes.-
THE END

Written by: Author and Poet
Robert E Rhines
10-31-2017

Father I'm in your hands keep me safe from harm or let me fight...
Amen Brothers and Sisters

Eternity

Could you spend eternity, intensely burning,-
Ages are turning.-

The numbers go by,-
Year after year you try.-

A lifetime is spent,-
Youth came, youth went.-

You still see what the reflections show,-
Wisdom comes, but never goes,-

But you can pass it second hand,-
Passed on, passed by you, it surely can.-

Before the time is through, with the blink of an eye,-
Youth is gone, life passed you by.-

Get to putting it out, straight,-
Simplicity of things, answers beyond fate.-

Go rest your mind, body sleep well,-
Tomorrow break the chains, do tell.-

My thoughts wandering, here ever after,-
Could anything be changed, would it, does it matter.-

Keep your thoughts simple, wait on nothing, for time is
not waiting on you,-
Baptise your inner sanctum your mind and your outer
body too.-

God raise us up, with your healing hands,-
We are all your children, oh Father of the lands.-

THE END

Written by: Author and Poet
Robert E Rhines
January 29, 2018
Copyright applies

End of the Day

Over it, with my head held high,-
Laughing, cause I'm worth more, and I don't have to try.-

For today is my day,-
More to do, less to say.-

But simply, I want to point out,-
Loss of compassion, loss of love and the loss of peace,
leaving doubt.-

Humanity is chained to society,-
Society is chained to anxiety.-

But none the less, life goes on,-
Its always darkest, before the dawn.-

Does it take humanity, to regain faith, in ones heart?-
Or is faith, not there from the start?-

Break the chains that bind all doubt,-
Let the compassion, let the caring, and let the love out.-

More energy is spent for the wrong,-
Come on, turn it around.-

Bring your shinning light forth,-
Open your hearts more.-

For the ones in the world, who don't know right,-
For the ones hungry, for the ones empty inside.-

It's not about what we have, or what we can gain,-
It's about piece of mind, peace in the hearts, at the end
of the day.-

THE END

Written by: Author and Poet
Robert E Rhines
March 1, 2018
Copyright applies

Everyday Peace

Working all day, in the summer sun,-
Then I'm ready, for the evening to come.-

I get alittle something to eat,-
I get my girls, a little treat.-

Anywheres better than, sitting at home,-
Busy on my phone.-

Take my girls, out for some evening air,-
Alittle fun time, run time, it's only fare.-

For all they give to me,-
A friendship, and security.-

Put down those cigs, put down the beers,-
You know how it works, your years.-

Times at hand,
Time is here,-
Actions speak louder than words, everyday peace, or
everyday fear.-

Get up, go out,-
Walk about.-

It's your health,-
Not your wealth.-

Though money can find a way to ease,-
Let your soul breathe, let your mind, your heart, find every day peace.-

Imprisoned from things, you have no control,-
I'm worth it, your worth it, believe it's all I know.-

Don't stay suspended in that time, let it go, let it pass you by,-
I've lived it, been there, want advice?? I'm that go to guy.-

THE END

Written by: Author and Poet
Robert E Rhines
February 1, 2018
Copyright applies

Final Rest

How can I tell you, things to sad, to be told,-
The helplessness of loss, in your arms grows cold.-

Maybe you could not tell,-
For the sickness inside of me, hidden so well.-

I don't know how you'll behave,-
Know that I am saved.-

You followed my casket,-
Questions in the balance, you should of asked it.-

You waited, perched above my grave,-
My final resting place.-

Can you imagine, how I felt that day,-
The final words, I never heard you say.-

You placed one final kiss upon my box,-
Hand full of dirt, hand full of rocks.-

If you really love me, and I think you do,-
These are my final words, true.-

Sit down beside me, take my hand,-
You feel the cold now, I was your man.-

Say friend, I came to listen,-
Reaching out for my hand now, it's gone, it's missin.

But if by chance, you shed a tear,-
I've had a wonderful life, a wonderful year.-

Til that day, your really old,-
Reach out for my hand now, before it turns cold.-

These are my words, I bared my soul,-
Final rest, it's to late, I feel it, I'm going home.-

THE END

Written by: Author and Poet
Robert E Rhines
February 5, 2018
Copyright applies

ire Storm

Brush, bushes and acres of trees,-
I am part of a fire crew, yeah a hot shot team.-

First on the scene,-
Head on into the fire storm, I mean.-

We fall the trees, that burn,-
Watching the winds, so if the fire storm turns.-

Cutting fire lines and trails as we go,-
Hard work, hot work and sweaty, breathing in the
smoke.-

We work as hard and as fast as we can,-
To preserve life in the land.-

Trying to save homes, where you live,-
Relentless and ruthless, a fire storm takes and never
gives.-

The fire storm rages and roars,-
Wild fire fighters, fighting fire storms.-

Winds change, fire surrounds,-
Dig in, fire blankets out, on the ground.-

Putting our lives on the line,-
Fire storm breaks out, here we go, one more time.-

Unforgiving, no remorse,-
Fighting fire storms.-

THE END

Written by: Author and Poet
Robert E Rhines
February 8, 2018
Copyright applies

For Love

Set your kiss, upon mine, the gleam in your eyes sparkle,-
Give yourself a moment, translucent a time to marvel.-

You do not need to rescue your touch, it goes against not
the boundaries.-

For Love ......

Your smiles, radiantly glows, brings forth the warmth
of the room,-
Be tempted, but not by just any man, softly and gently,
yet true.-

For Love ......

Set in your mind, a time, mesmerized in tranquility of
the touch,-
A tickle in the sense, remembrance of this name.-

For Love ......

Set your hand true, a brush, a tug pulling you, into
a smile, times gentle, times guidance, yet boundaries
between two broken.-

For Love ......

Set forth in boredom, and yet a guiltless clue,-
As you set your eyes upon mine if you dare.-

For Love......

THE END

Written by: Author and Poet
Robert E Rhines
February 16, 2018

Fourth of July

Early in the evening, the bonfires high,-
Barbeques a goin, beers on ice.-

Every day is the fourth of July,-
Shoot your rockets into the sky.-

Lighter in one hand,-
In the other a 16 oz bud can.-

Tip em up, toss em on back,-
Who cares about the time, when were out here, who's
keeping track.-

Radios blasting that great country sound,-
We play it all night, real loud.-

Kenny Chessney, to the Alman brothers band,-
Rocking it, barefoot in the sand.-

For all you, that crashed out early,-
Got to buzzed, on suds, or a little squirrelly,-

You'll wake up early, your head will feel dence,-
Whatever you did last night, won't make sense.-

Let's just say, you rock, rock good,-
Your always welcome out on the river, out in the woods.

As long as the weather is fine,-
Everyday is the fourth of July.-

Jump in your truck's, roll on out,-
Out that country road, line in the water, fishin for trout.-

Bonfires blazing, ice cold cans,-
Turn up the music, barefoot in the sand.-

We're all careful, nobody drives,-
Everyday is the fourth of July.-

Barbecued chicken, taste so right,-
With a tall can, cold as ice.-

Drinking responsible, no questions why,-
Live it, love it fourth of July.-

THE END

Written by: Author and Poet
Robert E Rhines
January 25, 2018

Going Through It

I open my eyes, to blue skies,-
Going through it, tears sting my eyes.-

I not only see things I hear things well,-
Going through it, how long, I can't tell.-

I pass on thoughts, that have know clue,-
Going through it, much easier with you.-

I'm feeling much better, you make me,-
Going through it, nothing's for free.-

I go to rest, it's all dark,-
Going through it, my dogs two bark.-

We wake far from the same,-
Going through it, in his name.-

We're on the same page,-
Going through it, is different, better with age.-

It's really different, from before,-
Going through it, in all ways good, for sure.-

I don't think I have felt this good,-
Going through it, knock like as in, on wood.-

I am saying, just saying,-
Going through it, blessings and still praying.-

I pray for you all,-
Standing tall.-
Going through it, well!!
Can't enjoy the heavenly things til you endure hell.-

THE END

Written by: Author and Poet
Robert E Rhines
December 21, 2017
Copyright applies

Grandpa

Hello grandpa, you don't know me or my name,-
I never met you either, just the same.-

You were gone, before I was ever born,-
At a young age, your liver worn.-

Not sure of year, you passed away,-
Grandpa, if I ever had a chance, these are the words,
I'd say.-

I never got to feel your hands on my hair, saying atta boy,-
Or run to you, when I broke my toy.-

I never got the chance, to talk,-
Or help you, when you got to old to walk.-

I never got the chance, to show you, i can throw a ball,-
Or hear you tell me, be a big boy, when I'd take a fall.-

I never got a chance, to have you teach me to drive,-
Or see your face, when you were alive.-

I never got the chance, to learn how to fish and hunt,-
Or let you see me fight others, and kick butt.-

I never got to hear you, tell me about the girls,-
Or take your old truck, for a whirl.-

Maybe when I get, to paradise, you know that place,-
I'll be able to see you, not just the picture of your face.-

And then again, do the things we never got to,-
Grandpa, I love you.-
I didn't have you grandpa, someday I might,-
Every grandkid should, have a grandpa, right??

THE END
Written by: Author and Poet
Robert E Rhines
January 14, 2018

Gun In Hand

Gun in hand, it's not fun, it's just sad, you'll see, -
The world isn't messed up that bad, it's just me.-

Gun in hand, ooh I feel, like I'm so big, -
Grave after grave we begin to dig. -

Gun in hand, makes me feel bigger, -
Mess with me, all I do is pull the trigger. -

Gun in hand, is not a time to play, -
No paper targets around, hunting season closed,
innocent lives lost on this day. -

Gun in hand, I couldn't go to war, -
Instead of suicide, it's now a game, let's see how I score. -

Gun in hand, will it ever be, over and done, -
So many deaths, what's in their heads, they think its
fun. -

Gun in hand, is just a gun, -
Until the thoughts of killing, something or someone. -

Gun in hand, think I'll go to hell, -
May God forgive me, if not, oh well.

THE END

Written by : Author and Poet
Robert E Rhines
November 8 2017

Hanging On

Hang in the balance, hang in its mast,-
I stand in the shadows, the reflections, the lights cast.-

No longer afraid,-

I hide no more,-

Standing up for me,-

I never did before.-

Hang on to truth, hang on to its word,-
I come from the shadows, my emptiness cured.-

No longer a weakness,-

I run no more,-

Stand for what I believe,-

It never mattered before.-

Hang there, and the world will soon see,-
I have come many miles, with weights, they have
burdened me.-

I will no longer stay silent,-

My voice will be heard,-

I will aspire to be a great writer, I poise for tolerance,-

I will let you hang in the balance, hang with every word.-

THE END

Written by: Author and Poet
Robert E Rhines
February 14, 2018
Copyright applies

Hold your own

A spin off or sequel,-
Better than, less than or equal.-

Real talk, real times and friends,-
Hang out, playful, fun times we spend.-

Someone lively, funny makes it go,-
Trial is an option, life is mysterious, one just don't know.-

Buzzed, listening aware of all around me,-
Wishing the future in advance, I could see.-

If the ride is long, if the ride is good,-
Beware though, I'm like rough cut wood.-

Take me, as a man,-
Real man, I am.-

Rock it, roll it, let nature run,-
Life is meant for happiness, happy times, laughter
and fun.-

It's not always a party, drinking and smoking bud,-
But when were off the road, back forty 4x4s in the mud.-

Messed up, falling out, passing out, not cool,-
Nothing makes sense, your starting to drool.-

You get up, you Bob and weave and bounce off the wall,-
Of my tires, then you trip, going down, flat on your face,
ends your fall.-

I'll give you this much, you can hold your own,-
Your a rider, don't give in, don't give up, throw up, and
go home.-

THE END

Written by: Author and Poet
Robert E Rhines
February 4, 2018

I Have Seen

I Have Seen, my share of the darkness,-
Mishaps, wrong decisions, creating a huge mess.-

I Have Seen, alot of places,-
Stared into the eyes of many faces.-

I Have Seen, the real, the fake,-
Heartfelt wanting to help, repeat of the same mistake.-

I Have Seen, miracles lots of trauma,-
Heard the lies, he said, she said, caught up in others drama.-

I Have Seen, the wrong, and witnessed the right,-
Stayed in the shadows, when you offered me your light.-

I Have Seen, the seasons change, they come, they go,-
Learning more everyday, everyday I grow.-

I Have Seen, the good, the bad,-
Learning through your eyes, now that I'm a Dad.-

I Have Seen, the happiness, the gloom,-
Not getting out of bed, not leaving my room.-

I Have Seen, your imaginary face,
Your in control, I am whole, through your grace.-

Amen Father, I was born a sinner,-
Walking with you, I am just a beginner.-
Blessed be in your name,-
Through you, we all have the power to change.-

THE END

Written by: Author and Poet ;
Robert E. Rhines
November 2017

Lost

Lost, messages and phone calls, on the waves of the air,-
Lost, my fingers while i stroke your hair.-

Lost, your body next to mine,-
Lost, the sweetness, and comfort, for a time.-

Lost, in your touch,-
Lost, me lost you, this much.-

Lost, lips soft kiss,-
Lost, without you, you I miss.-

Lost, but I see your face,-
Lost, remembering it's you I taste.-

Lost, a moment's rest,-
Lost, now I'm a mess.-

Lost, looking into your eyes,-
Lost, truthfully no lies.-

THE END

Written by: Author and Poet
Robert E Rhines
December 12, 2017
Copyright applies

I MISS YOU

I miss you, you know how, I came to be,-
You put, so much into me.-

I miss you, you know who, I am,-
You taught me, respect, fortitude, yes'sir yes'sir mam.-

I miss you, every single day,-
You never, got to see, me again but, you remember the
last, words I'd ever get to say.-

I miss you, you were there through it all,-
Even my coach, taught me baseball.-

I miss you, more and more as time goes on,-
Can't believe, I blinked and poof you were gone.-

I miss you, my hero, my best friend,-
No doubt, in my heart, you loved me, til the end.-

I miss you, alone my greatest journey has begun,-
Thank you Father in heaven
Daddy on earth, who am I ??
I miss you, this is your SON.....love you
I miss you.

THE END

Written by: Author and Poet
Robert E.Rhines
Twelve years gone
3 - 21-2006
Wrote this for you

Impact of loss

Loss is a feeling, in others I can't describe,-
It's unfairness, it's painful, it's hard at times.-

It's not really a feeling, but an impact,-
Meant to test us, throw us off, sideways or upside down,
infact.-

Loss is something unfair,-
It's selfish, it's cold it happens when we're unaware.-

It's something we all have endured,-
And some say time is the only cure.-

We mourne at some point, we fall apart, inside mostly,
for real,-
Meant to be broken, meant to be healed -

An impact, not planned, unwanted,-
But the aftermath, our thoughts haunted.-

We just have to learn, to adjust,-
Deal with it, find the strength inside us.-

With time, it heals everything, at least it's been said,-
Is it fact or fiction, the loss in your head.-

Loss is worse, when it's intended,-
Turn it over to God, because time alone won't mend it.-

THE END

Written by: Author and Poet
Robert E Rhines
February 7, 2018
Copyright applies

Independent

The day's of ole, or the old days,-
Old school, OG, and old ways.-

My, things have changed dramatically,-
Some for the good, some for the worse, ironically.-

From buildings, to cars,-
From music, to Bar's.-

Taking our religion out of our schools,-
My, things have gone to far, treated like fools.-

From overseas trade,-
From pledging to our country, our flags being hated.-

The future of this country, is at hand,-
Something needs to be done, if it can.-

My, things have and continue to slide,-
Some things, with no attempt to hide.-

The sad story's from 9-11 and other tragedies long past,-
And damages amount beyond, mass.-

My, things have been buried away,-
The hole gets deeper, by the day.-

From lies and deceit,-
From first timers, others a repeat.-

The tragedies, the loss of life,-
Sustained with the innocent, plotting outright.-

My, things have taken its toll,-
The government gets a grade A for there roll.-

From the internal affairs,-
From the FBI, CIA anyone really care.-

The foreign policy's are a joke,-
Can any of it be stopped, one should hope.-

My, things have been put into the wrong hands,
That goes out to all you politicians.-

From gas stations with mini Mart's,
From truck drivers and taxi cars.-

The days, our yesterday's, our culture, being put to rest,-
My, things in America, what a mess.-

From un voted laws,-
From over population, a shortage of jobs.-

Independent I am,- independent I'll be,-
Until America is America again, agreed.-

THE END

Written by: Author and Poet
Robert E Rhines
January 23, 2018
Copyright applies

Innocence lost

From the broken homes, or the homes at peace,-
To the emptiness of the wandering streets.-

Once cheerful laughter, now tormented cries,-
Unforseen pain, holds no lies.-

Utter in silence,-
For the shame, for the violence.-

We counted the happiness, at tremendous cost,-
For the unseen brutality, mistreatment of youth,
innocence lost.-

Screams for help, a hand silent,-
Dreams broken, the traumas violent.-

We the people, parents must protect,-
Our children, from the molestation, the killing, the
drugs, what's next.-

We've had our eyes closed,-
Now human trafficking has a rose.-

Our churches, people in office, to our schools,-
It's gone way far, for to long, we look like fools.-

Molesting our children, to raping unwanted affairs,-

Hang em from a rope, right then, right there.-

Laws slap there hands, back on the street,-
Another child, another victim, a sickness they can't
overcome, they can't beat.-

A rope and a tree,-
Honest words spoken, as a boy, it happened to me.-

Laughter is gone, no smile on your face,-
Until we rid the evil, restore innocence, to its rightful
place.

THE END

Written by: Author and Poet
Robert E Rhines
February 9, 2018
Copyright applies

 *I Stand*

I Stand for, the red,white and the blue,-
What color of flag, flies for you.-

It's not, the color of flag you fly,-
Or a difference of blood in your veins, or the tear in
your eye.-

I Stand for, the red, white and the blue,-
Not for the government, trying to control the people like
me, like you.-

You can't help, but see all the wrong,-
And most of us, have known all along.-

I Stand for, the red, white and the blue,-
To me it's not, the country your from, it's about what's
true.-

All along they hide secrets, we bury the innocent at the
church, with a tall steeple,-
The government don't care about
"we the people".-

I Stand for, always the red, white and the blue,-
I'm for the people, "we the people"....... And you.-

Right is right, but so much wrong,-

"We the people" let it go for to long.-

I Stand for, the free red, white and the blue,-
But standing by, while the government, keeps doing what they do.-

Ask not what your country can do, for you,-
But what you can do for your country, and get buried ....
it's true.-

I Stand for, the strong red, white and the blue,-
Government corruption way back in the Lincoln days, a story I'll share, with you.-

For the government was not built on deceitful acts, or mountains of lie's,-
Private contractor's, paid assassins or spies.-

I Stand for, the brave, all over the Americas, foreign countries population control people die,-
In the news, social media, I hear it, but can't open my eyes.-

I Stand for, the proud and tall, red, white and the blue,-
It begins with the people like me, and people like you.-

Stand with me, for what is right,
Or die with me, but it was a hell of a good fight.

THE END

Written by: Author and Poet,
Robert E. Rhines
Nov. 15 th 2017

All Gone

I see it as this, evil, getting even, its not me either is pay back,-
Thoughts of verbally striping you, not your clothes, your self worth, esteem, things like that.-

Mind twisting you, so you can't really think,-
There's an excuse for you, earlier now, start, have a drink.-

Nothing mean or nasty, to you, or about you, can make you come close, to the pain I feel,-
Coldest to ever cross my path, that I've met, but hey, not a big deal.-

Your a liar, fat mouth, to be heard, you got to be loud,-
Does it make your momma and your daddy good parent's, and proud.-

I'd tell them, how much of a joke you are,-
And that's where you get your release, the bar.-

One step above the low ender,-
Drinking more and more, it's a mind bender.-

Though i called it, early on account of your baggage, close to over size,-
And thinking you can hide it, behind your eyes.-

Nothing serious would ever be in your cards,-
Bleach blonde hair, nasty demeanor pushing people
to far.-

You'll get lit up one day or at night,-
Beat down in 2.2, weak and running your mouth, you
can't win a fight.-

Your mouth is just as bad, writing checks, your ass can't
cash,-
Someone is going to take it wrong, and have an anger
problem, smash.-

Them teeth won't need pulled, busted out, broke,-
Laugh about it now, later you won't see it as a joke.-

Gold digger, step up player,-
Before to long, back on the street, it's getting colder out,
put-on an extra layer.-

I am positive about this, run your game on ones not so
smart,-
You could get a whoopin, just to start,-

Gone, I'm out in a few days, leaving this shit hole,-
There's nothing I will do for you now, this man's gotta roll.-

THE END

Written by: Author and Poet
R.E.Rhines
Sept 26,2017

A- Cat's Everywhere

Along the river bottoms rocky or of sand,-
No difference if it's woman or man.-

From the bushes that camouflage all there faces,-
Sidewalk sitters, dumpster divers pushed from all
spaces.-

Baggy clothes stained from the dirt beneath there feet,-
Mismatched, tore back,and raggy standing in line
to eat.-

City being swarmed in droves of the misunderstood,
misfits all homeless and unfortunate ones,-
From all the hidden spots they all show after daylight
fades, gone.-

From levy to levy trees cut down bushes taken away,-
The jungle don't even look the same today.-

Children suffer from no fault of there own,-
Traumatized as children and stays even after there
grown.-

No regular security or stability of a home nor beds being
soft as they sleep,-
From one day to the next possessions they gather and
keep.-

Some drug addicts, alcoholics and mentally ill making a mess everywhere they go,-
No care of where there garbage they throw.-

It's almost like a plague of rats in the sewers,-
The cities being uprooted and baron from all talkers no doers.-

Orchard's, empty fields way out in the woods hiding there camps,-
Out of sight but not mind darkness brings them out like vamps.-

Most of them live for there addiction from day to day,-
In there own worlds nothing important accomplished thats there way.

THE END

Written by: author and poet
Mr R.E.Rhines
SEPT 18,2017

esus Say's

Come take my hand, little girl,-
I'm the father of the world.-

Let me take you, where there's no more pain,-
No more strangers, you'll know every name.-

A paradise true, there's no others,-
Free from all the stains in the world, all sister's and
brothers.-

No more bad tongues, no hurt feelings,-
No more dying, no more killings.-

Come take my hand, follow me,-
I'm the father of the world, Jesus I say to thee.-

Let me show you, a paradise so profound,-
Where no evil lurks, no yelling, no crying sound.-

A paradise true,-
Let's walk, I'll walk with you.-

No more sickness, no colds,-
No more death from getting old.-

Come take my hand, walk with me,-
There's nothing, I don't know, nothing i don't see.-

Let's walk the road paved in gold, see it's shine,-
Where the halos, are bright, oh child of mine.-

No more ugliness, shall you see,-
Now take my hand, and walk with me.-

I am the father of the world, this is what I say,-
Here you are safe.-

THE END

Written by: Author and Poet
Robert E Rhines
January 25, 2018
Copyright applies

No more homeless, no more rent

Let Me

Will you let me, be the man, to love you, like no other,-
A better love, unlike a father or brother.-

Will you let me, take you in my arms, in the night, and
hold you,-
Keeping you wrapped up, not in my arms alone, but a
fairytale love....true.-

Will you let me, protect you and keep you always, safe
from harm,-
Snuggled right next to me, all comfortable warm.-

Will you let me, sweep you off your feet,-
After the lights go out, settle on down, all nice and neat.-

Will you let me, love you unconditionally,-
Sometimes serious, sometimes silly.-

Will you let me, ask you, take my hand,-
God's law, make me an honest man.-

Will you let me, love you from now, til our end,-
Honestly, trusting, caring and best friend.-

Will you let me, spoil you, or give all I can,-
And no matter what, you'll never long, for another man.-

THE END

Written by: Author/ Poet
Robert E. Rhines
11-6-2017

ittle or Lot

Like it a little or a lot,-
Time won't stay forever, though we think it's all we got.-

Far away stars, look down and shine,-
Guiding souls, your soul to mine.-

We'll not always agree,-
Communication, compromise, understanding is key.-

Aimlessly lost a traveler on the wind,-
A new beginning, beginning, not an end.-

Loneliness knocked on my heart, tried to settle,-
It was hard, usually I am care free and gentle.-

Til sadness came, tried to take over,-
What intervened was you, not luck, a rabbit's foot, huh,
four leaf clover.-

Like it a little or a lot,-
Not loaded with riches, far from hot.-

Big heart, you get what you see,-
It's about choices, choices like me.-

Decisions based on a choice,-

The sound of birds in distance singing, back up to your voice.-

Happiness has come in like a storm, no damage but a smile sits in its place,-
Sounds in my own voice, see it upon this face.-

Loyalty now takes hold, now has a hand,-
From the soul of a woman, soul of a man.-

Honor boasts, it's set up on my chest,-
I won't promise you the world, but I'll do my best.-

Its making it through, there's no bust,-
Cardboard sign reads faith in him, faith in us...

Life, love and happiness is a powerful thing,-
Nothing positively says it better than a ring.-
Is that your phone????

THE END

Written by: Author and Poet
Robert E Rhines
Special thanks to my friend......
Tail end of 2017

Judgments a "comin"

Get closer to God, closer to faith,-
No need, no reason, to be ashamed.-

Put your hands in the air, receive him, rejoice,-
Rise up, sing and dance, make some noise.-

Don't sit there, stand there alone,-
The King of Kings, Lord Almighty, our creator, time
is born.-

Thank him, in his name we praise,-
Once again, from death he will raise.-

The trumpets sound, the Angels sing,-
Our Lord is returning, our Father the King.-

He created the heavens, he created the earth,-
A baby in a manger, a King from birth.-

Simple instructions, an uneducated guess,-
Deliver us from evil, our transgressions, sins confess.-

Our Father in heaven, give us our daily bread,-
Two loaves, five thousand were fed.-

Drink this, the blood of Christ,-
Wash away your sins, cleanse yourself, baptised.-

Come all you sinners, behold,-
Saved, walk the city paved in gold.-
Since I was a child, this stories been told.-

Receive his love, praise his name,-
A sin is a sin, but no sin the same.-

Rise up look now,-
Judgment days a comin, his wrath is comin, down.-

THE END

Written by: Author and Poet
Robert E Rhines
February 1, 2018
Copyright applies

Let me not Sway

Let me set eyes upon you, let me be intrigued, your beauty, your radiant hair.
Your a shimmering light, a ray of hope, as the smile sets upon your face.
Let me not Sway......

Let me bask in your love, come yet another day, your laughter renders me helpless in moments like these.
Your a guiding light, when I am lost, a candle set forth in the windows, I am not me, when I ask you for a taste.
Let me not Sway.....

Let me forever stand true, exuberant, masculine before you, succumb to nature, a beast I am. Grounds for this haunted heart.
Let me not Sway......

Beautiful as is the words, well written in everyway.
Let me find truth in Love, like a flower, yet I shall not pass.
Let me not Sway......

Time is all proof, for the words to come, feast not on there meanings, yet on the love that comes only once.
Let me not be inadequate, for my senses are gone, remembrance of our song.
Let me not Sway......

THE END

Written by: Author and Poet
Robert E Rhines
February 14, 2018
Copyright applies

Look down on Me

I've battled myself, the worst of enemies,-
Consequences of my own actions, severe altercations
don't remedy.-

The fears never seen, I hold inside,-
Stained from the pain, the remembrance i hide.-

My heart feels, what my eyes can't see,-
Look down on me.-

Now I'm brought from self-destruction, beginnings of
a new road,-
With you beside me,- not behind me,-
You unburden my heart, you lightened my load.-

And brings back the selflessness, the righteous smile,-
Jesus if it pleases, look down on me, for alittle while.-

Knowing what my heart feels, what my mouth don't
speak, I'm sorry,-
Sit, let me back, in the warmth of your glory.-

Where the sorrow once stained,-
A heart filled with hate, your love remained.-

Look down on me,-
You stayed through it all, was I to blind to see.-

You brought me back from the depths, darkest of days,-
Out of the clutches of evil, my pitiful ways.-

As you know, I don't hold Ill will towards others, but myself in contempt,-
For the path, I knew wrong, an air in judgements.-

My eyes are wide open, now I see,-
Look down on me.-

THE END

Written by: Author and Poet
Robert E Rhines
February 10, 2018
Copyright applies

Love and loyalty

Love and loyalty knows no bounds,-
From a friend, who is sound.-

You stand next to a friend, who holds visions,-
Next to a friend, that has no problems expressing, no
problems, and listens.-

With love from the heart, full of internal pride,-
Loyalty and friendship, no demons to hide.-

Before the sunsets, the weather's dry,-
Go ahead with laughter, no tears to cry.-

But those of joy,-
A friend true, inside and outside, not lost once like
the boy.-

Takes a long look, into your eyes, and stares,-
Love in the heart, loyalty and reasons, and cares.-

Mesmerized in the tranquility of your eyes,-
Not fascinated in others, or preoccupied.-

He stands before you, now go forth,-
Your own love and loyalty of course.-

Return to him, what is given,-
It's time now, start liven.-

There's no love, or loyalty that compares,-
From a friend, who stands right there.

THE END

Written by: Author and Poet
Robert E Rhines
February 3, 2018
Copyright applies

ove Strong

Love Strong,-
You can't measure it, other than time will tell, if you belong.-

Hearts grow fond,-
It's right? It's wrong.-

A sense of security, minds ponder on,-
Emotional duress, fictional stress, Love beyond.-

Love built on, integrity, respect and honor, but when it's gone!!-
Reckless feelings, emptiness pains the heart, it's more than over, it's past done.-

Simply, thoughtfulness, a solution, take time to embrace, and your time is now, Hun,-
No time is ever better than the present, your times begun.-

Hold em, Love em, please em, like there the only one,-
Whisper to em, call em, tell em loud, have fun!!-

Love Strong,-
This is where you belong.-

It's been a hell of a run, been fun, nothing's wrong,-
No thoughts to ponder, or let your mind wander, beyond.-

Love em, lead em, guild em, hard work is never done,-
Friends til the end, our times just begun.-

Respect em, be nice, tolerate em, never hate em, don't say
or do things that can't be undone,-
Love Strong,-
The only one.-

THE END

Written by: Author and Poet
Robert E Rhines
February 22, 2018
Copyright applies

Made by you

From the start, the very beginning,-
Made by you, your image, not for sinning.-

These hands, strong and sound,-
Made by you, a carpenter found.-

My eyes, set to read the words in your book,-
Made by you, not to judge or cast a dirty look.-

A mind full of talents, where do I start,-
Made by you, kindness and love in this heart.-

Mouth full of words, through you the poetry flows,-
Made by you, caring emotions, and it shows.-

Hand full of dirt you created man,-
Made by you, from your hand.-

Set from the same beginning, I broke laws,-
Made by you, perfect in my eyes, others see flaws.-

Two legs and feet,-
Made by you, with a breath, with a heart beat.-

Not always wrong, not always right,-
Made by you, flesh of the body, wisdom of the mind,
soul of your light.-

You've given me so much, I have given way less,-
Made by you, I've done wrong, I will repent, I will
confess.-

y Mind

I hear the choppers chasing over head,-
Sandman's torturing me, waking soaked, in bed.-

Gun fire ricocheting, sounds off the foothills,-
Taking bets, on misses, hits and kills.-

Tracing uncharted steps in the gravel, dust and sand,-
Over thinking, stay alive, on the other hand .-

Out of the Lz, on a routine work detail,-
Adjusting to a team, overcome, adapt, you will not fail.-

Scouting around, radios blasting sound,-
Locked and loaded, hit the ground.-

Try to get my berings, find the shot,-
Only my mind thinks, not.-

Like a repeat, over again, broken record on replay,-
My mind, I fight this every day.-

The uniform I wore was ROTC,-
I didn't think it was for me.-

Cursed for not doing my part,-
A burden I now carry in my heart.-

My share of battles,-
Quick like a snake, not a sound, no rattles.-

This is my mind,-
On and on, constant rewind.-

My brother's I feel your pain,-
Every man that falls next to you, remember every name.-

THE END

Written by: Author and Poet
Robert E Rhines
December 26, 2017
Copyrights apply

My Prayers

Oh Father in heaven, I know you exist,-
My prayers to you, on things that need fixed.-

I pray for the weak, may they grow strong,-
For the world to get along.-

I pray for the rich, to help the poor,-
For everyone to sleep in a warm bed, not on the floor.-

I pray for this country, and the next,-
For the devastation and the lives mother nature wrecks.-

I pray for world hunger to end,-
No matter the skin color, white, brown, black or red.-

I pray for the addict's, that need or don't need a fix,-
For the bullies, who get there kicks.-

I pray for more laughter, less pain,-
For all to receive you, and praise your name.-

I pray for the less fortunate, no doubt,-
For the ones in prison, that'll never get out.-

I pray for all my sisters, my brothers,-
For my Dad, for my mother's,

I pray this in your name,-
For this is my prayers, day in, day always the same.-

Amen...Amen... Amen

THE END

Written by: Author and Poet
Robert E Rhines
January 13, 2018
Copyright applies

My Song

Get up, early morning sunrise,-
Go for a walk in the drizzling rain, water in my eyes.-

Lightning flashes, thunder booms,-
Cool winds across the lake, with the sounds of lunes.-

Trees sway back and forth,-
From the south to the north.-

Broken halos plays on the radio,-
The song touches my soul,-

I break the silence, the sound of my voice,-
Singing it loud.....
Singing it proud....
Just one of the good ole boys.-

Music, on and on it plays,-
The beat, the rhythm the trees sway.-

Every other sound,-
Feet stomping the ground.-

Nothing wrong, about a great tune,-
Or my wet hair, in the early morning dew.-

Keep the music real, attend to life,-
Music good for the soul, day or night.-

Turn it up, sing along,-
Ease your soul, when your feeling wrong.-

THE END

Written by: Author and Poet
Robert E Rhines
January 10, 2018
Copyright applies

Next Life

It's like, time in a bottle, a note drifting at sea,-
I whisper your name, louder still, you don't hear me.-

Standing off in the distance, well in the shadows,-
The days to come, the lost tomorrow's.-

Silence falls on a def ear,-
Beating of a heart, faintly, you do not hear.-

Pounding, not in your own chest,-
The weight of a head, laying as you rest.-

Again softly, boom, boom,-
The only sound inside, this room.-

With bodies all snuggled in, warm and cozy,-
It's cold, see my breath, a nose red, cheeks Rosey .-

Stopping again, rustling done,-
Listening for another, boom, boon, it doesn't come.-

Freeze motionless, waiting, not one sound,-
Blankets pulled back, knees to the ground.-

Father in heaven, not the girl, take me the boy,-
She's done so much good, brought so much joy.-

If ever I'm laying there, gone, I've passed by,-
Be stronger than ever, I'm waiting for you my love, in
the next life.-

THE END

Written by; Author and Poet:
Robert E. Rhines
November 2017

Nightmare solutions

Tossing and turning, kicking and screaming,-
Nightmares lurk, evils dreaming.-

Madness looms in your head,-
If you don't clear your thoughts before bed.-

Your thoughts go evil, dreams get crazy,-
Imaginations run ramped, your minds wild, faith gets hazy.-

Take your mind,-
To a happier time.-

Cause if you go to bed mad,-
Your thoughts are mean, your dreams get bad.-

You'll wake up, sheets soaking wet,-
Coughing, choking, trying to catch your breath.-

So before you lay down for sleep,-
Ask the Lord, your soul to keep.-

Let your mind wander, your thoughts stay free,-
And go to sleep, have good dreams.-

Or go to bed, with twisted thought's, and your mind
is mad,-
Your feeling of emptiness, lost or sad.-

Watch your dreams, not of happiness, or being fulfilled,-
But of anger, mass destruction, or people killed.-

Meditation is a form of prayer, it clears your body, and
your mind,-
And your nightmares, turns into dreams, true happiness
you will find.-

Lord I pray unto you, if I should pass before I awake,-
My soul is yours to take.-

THE END

Written by: Author and Poet
Robert E Rhines
February 26, 2018

Not Made

Not Made, of steel or of wood,-
Feelings are hard, mainly misunderstood.-

Not Made, of materials like synthetic,-
If you can't tell, I am not of plastic.-

Not Made, of all simple things, alone,-
Hair, toes, and fingers, skin to cover the bone.-

Not Made, of all sugars sweetest and spice,-
Never closed off to the what ifs, nice.-

Not Made, of all patience, to quick to trust,-
There's a little broken in all of us.-

Not Made, of weakness, I know no fear,
Death has found me four times, I'm still here.-

Not Made, perfectly, far behind,-
Maybe not the brightest star, you see me shine.-

Life has its way, of handing out simplest journeys or the
harder quests,-
Don't stay broken, lost, confused in a world unsure like
the rest.-

Not Made for deceitful acts towards my fellow man,-
Secrets, sneaking around, lying is not who I am.-

Not Made, flawlessly,-
I am tarnished, I have faults, as imperfect, as imperfect
can be.-

Not Made for judging you or your judgement on me.......

THE END

Written by; Author and Poet
Robert E Rhines

h Father

Oh Father, I've fallen short, so many times,-
You've never turned your back on me, or left me behind.-

Oh Father, 10 commandments, your only law,-
I've sinned, yet miracles before me, not only in my life,
but in others, I saw.-

Oh Father, your grace,-
I've been blessed in seeing your face.-

Oh Father, I've been saved, washed clean by your blood,-
You've been sacrificed, died on the cross.-

Oh Father, I walk with you, here on out,-
Your word is the proof, left in me, there is no more doubt.-

Oh Father, keep your hand upon me, if I stumble, so I
won't fall,-
You've been put before us, your the strength in all.-

Oh Father, my personal journey is with you in my life,-
You've shown me my path, that road, is right.-

Oh Father, so it is written, so it shall be,- through you,
all things are possible, even for, sinners like me.
While I was in church on Sunday morning and the
words just came to mind. Amen

THE END

Written by : Author and Poet
Robert E. Rhines
10-29-2017

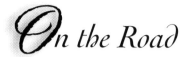n the Road

Somewheres between Arlington, Tennessee and San Antonio,
Hi- way 35, a long stretch of road,-

Translucent lights, blind some glimmering eyes.

On the Road.......

Fast-food, mini mart's, with gas pumps, along the many aways,-
On ramps and exits, used endlessly by thousands, affixed to there days.-

On the Road.....

Set out apart, no pre trip inspections, for myself I challenge,-
Destinations a to b guided by faith,-
In no hurry, to find myself anywhere, it's not my race,-
No predetermined schedule, no specific time zone.-

On the Road......

Open the eight,-
Hi- way 35, or interstate, almost 300 lost, this year to date,-

Only the second month of the year, be cautious, be careful and stay safe, let not the interstate 35 be your fate.-

On the Road......

THE END

Written by: Author and Poet
Robert E Rhines
February 16, 2018

Our Lord, Our God

I survived, I beat the odds,-
The damage, cancer can cause.-

Like others unfortunate,-
Some body's buried, others we cremate.-

Ashes to ashes,-
Here today, tomorrow your life flashes.-

Before your own eyes,-
Hold back the tears, inside nobody else sees you cry.-

The pain within you hold,-
Is it better for the young, better for the old.-

Life is beginning,-
Life is ending.-

Surviving is just another step,-
It makes none of us, better than the rest.-

When it seems all else has failed,-
On a mantel, in a box, or in a coffin your nailed.-

It's the power of Christ, through him you believe,-
It's your actions in life, it counts before you leave.-

Give it unto him, our Father in heaven,-
Let it be his will, though the pain is dwellin.

Strength comes from above,-
Courage to get past all, through his love.-

What you think, you bring about,-
There's no easy way out.-

Unless it is suicide,-
Purgatory is waiting, it's a slow ride.-

The fight we fight, to survive,-
And without him, what is life.-

Here today, gone tomorrow,-
Filled with pain and hatred, filled with sorrow.-

Live and let live,-
Love him, love others, receive blessings, for all you give.-

I am a survivor, one of the few,-
Open your hearts, love him as he loves you.-

I beat the odds,-
Not without the love of our Father, our God.-

THE END

Written by: Author and Poet
Robert E Rhines
January 11, 2018
Copyright applies

ver Again

Girls will be Girls, they drink, they holler,-
But these two are the best, I'll buy that for a dollar.-

Brandi's from Texas, Angie's from Kentucky,-
Couple of the coolest chic's, better than any ole rubber ducky.-

They'll get it the tub,-
They splish, they splash, they rub a dub, dub.-

Tonight rubber ducky, I think I'll have to pass,-
Me a Jonny's got a bottle and a full tank of gas.-

Going to pick up the girls, take them to dance,-
Dance in the dark, dance in the sheets, little midnight romance.-

There fun, when you get them to laughing,-
Throw on some country music, air guitars and knee slapping.-

There's no hair pulling, when these girls fight,-
They do it good, they do it right.-

Bottle is gone, it's time to fly,-
Bottle is gone, our mouths are dry.-

Friday night is over, time for Saturday to begin,-
Saturday night, we'll do it all over again.-

We stay out of town, we stay out of the bars,-
Out in the woods, music loud, under the stars.-

Jonny comes back with a bloody nose,-
Ran into a tree, the story goes.-

The truth hell no,-
We jump in the truck, it's time to go.-

Get these girls fired up on a bottle,-
Better be ready, there all out, full throttle.-

Foot to the floor, let the tires spin,-
We'll do it next weekend all over again.-

THE END

Written by: Author and Poet
Robert E Rhines
December 2, 2017
Copyright applies

Pointing back

You come with worry,-
Rattled judge, rattled jury.-

Judgement and blame,-
Pointing fingers, no shame.-

Resentment holds true,-
Regret binds you.-

Words without consent,-
Eyes full of regret.-

Mindful, seeking doubt,-
You open your mouth, truth holds out.-

Consequences you seek,-
Anger's raging, tempers peek.-

You do what you do,-
There's no fight, in you.-

Truths are tried,-
Resolutions, a powerless mind.-

Stop, calibration of facts,-
Sustained or overruled, both separate acts.-

Next time you point, at someone else, for what they do,-
Look at your own hand, three fingers pointing back
at you.-

THE END

Written by: Author and Poet
Robert E Rhines
February 3, 2018
Copyright applies

Pretty Eyes

It is the middle of September, when I entered her bar, for a beer,-
Absolutely a perfect day, for the rest of crap that's happened, this year.-

When I captured a glimpse and the essence, of her,-
Beautiful face, blond, first, yet she's natural, no kitten for sure.-

It took three or maybe four return trips, of going in there,-
Because I am shy, comfortable connection before conversation and I was ready to share.-

Then our eyes met,-
She replied, you hear this all the time, I bet.-

You have really pretty eyes,-
I said thank you, then, without reason toung tied.-

Imaginable but unforeseen aura, fascinating will and perfect,-
Gemini, head strong, alpha female, could be a dangerous matter of subject.-

As I begin to see her on a continued day after day,-
All the while, pretty eyes, she'd say.-

Even when she introduced her friends, to me,-
Pretty eyes, handsome ! Isn't he?-

Amongst her friends that's the intro,-
Even had me meet her family, as in, also parents, ooh no!!

Is she going to keep me around?-
Because of pretty eyes blue, not brown?-

Can state this, without doubt,-
We hook up, either of us won't have an easy out.-

Remember she's like the female twin,-
But no competition, ready, set begin.-

Something says she's solid, but it could mean danger,-
Two doubles, what could any more stranger.-

Steady as she goes,-
Not as in boats, or sail to catch the winds blow.-

Simple is not as it seems,-
No more nightmares, but all sweet dreams.-

Pretty eyes won't make a couple stand,-
And differences on views, opinions on the other hand.-

Close attention, give and receive, communication, trust,-
Believe in, back up, loyalty, a solid foundation a must.-

I'm not jumping ahead, nothing's set in stone,-

Though you like each other, companionship, both tired,
of being alone.-

Pretty eyes, just play by ear,-
Who knows it could be a good start at the end of the
worst year.-

Rare Elements

Conversations, crossed the paths on social media site,-
Truest of words, honesty spoke, sparks ignite.-

It's only been a few short weeks,-
The laughter, silliness sharing pain in our abs, to numbness in our cheeks.-

Rare Elements, of two,-
A connection, amazingly beautiful and true.-

Abundantly sent, blessings from heaven, I see that clear,-
Reaching for the stars, awesome beginning at the end of the year.-

Rare Elements, this intense, definitely rare find,-
Ones such as us, not one but two of a kind.-

Text messages of the hook, three hour phone calls,
It's like were in school again, writing on the black boards
" No running in the Halls"

The racing hearts, butterfly's, sweaty palm,-
Face to face meeting, get excited, no stay calm.-

It'll be hard once we touch,-
Overly excited, what's to much.-

Rare Elements, and the laughter is freed,-
You'll be the rider, and I your faithful steed.-

No not for hire, of course,-
A stud yes, but a man, not a horse.-

Staying true to who we are,-
Standing the tests of time, we'll go far.-

THE END

Written by; Author and Poet
Robert E Rhines

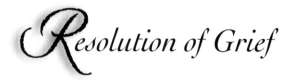 Resolution of Grief

Into a country, a war your born,-
Grief stricken, from the bodies worn.-

Some battles won, wars are lost,-
Death all around, a soldier's cost.-

Bravery and honor, won't stand alone,-
When a son, brother or father can't come home.-

Testify to the destruction, all you see,-
I pray for you, I'm gone pray for me.-

Dead, gone buried away,-
Never again to be seen, only my memories stay.-

Uniform all pressed, and true,-
A team, band of brothers, all's left is you.-

Your minds left in a horrific maze,-
Guns firing, explosions lost in a daze.-

A farewell letter passed on down,-
From the fallen, many places, a city, or town.-

Take back the fateful day at best,-
A love, for honor, in peace may you rest.-

Rollback, get some sleep,-
In my mind, I'm still in the fight, I pray my soul will keep.-

When I am gone, I never came home,-
I'm always with you, your never alone.-

My mind, my burdens, my flaws,-
War is for nothing, with out a cause.-

Remember me as the sunsets, or rises at dawn,-
You'll always have my memories, I am never gone.-

Love me, set me free,-
We'll walk in heaven, as it is written, it shall be.-

Love.....Live..... in Peace

THE END

Written by: Author and Poet
Robert E Rhines
December 7, 2017
For the Fallen
Copyright applies

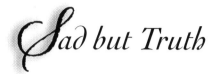ad but Truth

Hindering life, distorted youth,-
Facts laid before us, sad but truth.-

Compounding problems, insecurities on the rise,-
It's hard to see the evidence, to read there eyes.-

Easier to let it go, to difficult to try,-
Trust diminished, to many lives.-

Society has taken over, taken its toll,-
We've lost our children, trying to regain control.-

There's no punishment, all warnings,-
Our youth is corrupt, and blind we sit, idle by ignoring.-

Then we blame, it's to late,-
Where love once laid in there hearts, now stands hate.-

There's no time like now, it's present,-
We shouldn't bury our children, holding pain, mourning
discontent.-

To much free time, responsibilities end,-
Parents matter, then friend.-

Stay in tune, stay close,-
Staying in there business, is the only way to know.-

All of it sad but truth,-
Our hands are dirty now, anger abides inside our youth.-

THE END

Written by: Author and Poet
Robert E Rhines
February 9, 2018
Copyright applies

Satan

Satan's a knocking, on the weaknesses of mankind,-
Knocking on the doors, and preying on your mind.-

Satan's working overtime,-
Every vulnerable place in your life, except for yours,
except for mine.-

Dark Lord, no Lord at all,-
Our Lord will prevail, again Satan will fall.-

His time is at hand, as well, but until that day,-
All the weak, non believers, his followers, help him stay,-

Evil around everywhere lurks,-
Faith in the Father, believe it works.-

Believe in the only Lord, Jesus Christ, who art in the
heavens above,-
For Satan is pure evil, false promises, false Love.-

He was banished once, he lost,-
Stripped of his position, his wings though he fought.-

He preys on the weak hearts, weak minded the loners
of non believers,-
The liars, cheaters and the deceivers.-

Walk with him, with Satan in the dark, it'll come to an end,-
For the one Lord, our Lord is coming, returning again.-

Nothing about Satan is captivating, a eternity of damnation, endlessly burning in fire,-
For there is only one, God the Father, he holds a power higher.-

I'll pray for you now, save yourself, before it's to late,-
Broken is Satan, believe in nothing, suffer at his hands, his dark fate.-

THE END

Written by: Author and Poet
Robert E Rhines
February 5, 2018
Copyright applies

Seven letter word

There's a seven letter word,-
Thrown about, misused, a misconception, far from learned.-

We hear words used everyday,-
But adequate meanings are lost along the way.-

Like you feel it's owed, based on your name,-
Or because your a big shot, under estimation, but considered just the same.-

It's about " respect."-
Means more than its meaning in our simple dialect.-

It's a word that most of us learn, it's instilled, while we're young,-
But not implemented, but restricted by some.-

Here's the lesson learned,-
Respect is supposed to given, not earned.-

In the same aspect, some far from deserving,-
But disrespect them, kick up a storm, cause a scene, unnerving.-

There's and old proverb,-
That accompanies, this seven letter word.-

It goes like this,-
Respect others, respect yourself, that's how it is.-

If you don't respect yourself, how can others respect you?-
A seven letter word, it's about what you say, about what you do.-

THE END

Written by: Author and Poet
Robert E Rhines
February 10, 2018
Copyright applies

Shame is Lost

Though, I walk through these days to come, in this world of evils,-
You are now with me, for now I am a believer,-

I'm saved now, Jesus Christ, my redeemer,-
Many days lost, days I've walked alone, days I don't want to remember.-

I was off course, I was lost, I was broken, full of shame,-
And cried in self pity, in secret, when I heard your name.-

Utterly I would tremble, I would cry.-
With the thoughts, you spared me, what for, why??-

I took the roads, most travel,-
Until my life, began to deteriorate, at the point, it would unravel.-

You sent me an Angel, you have spared me, you saved my life,-
At the heights of my destruction, the most crucial of times.-

A man on the verge of death, on the edge of being lost forever,-
But to me you proved, with my prayers, any storm, can be weathered.-

Your guidance, you are the light in the storm,-
Blessings come in many forms.-

From putting your hands, on the souls lost,-
Miracles of life, or the life, is the cost.-

But you set me on an open course,-
It's not about the riches in this world, or about being poor.-

Though my past days, have been dark, lost, pitiful, filled in shame,-
Shame is lost now, receiving you, and I'm praising your name.-

THE END

Written by: Author and Poet
Robert E Rhines
February 12, 2018
Copyright applies

Signs

There are signs, for everything, there's signs for all,-
Caution signs, careful, watch your step or fall.-

There are large ones, small ones alike,-
Warning signs, pedestrians on a bike.-

There are huge ones, like the billboards,-
Neon ones that lite up our games, score.-

There are signs, flashing for the cross walk,-
Signs saying turn of your cellphone, shh no talk.-

There's signs for hospitals, for reserved parking,-
Paying attention, to the signs, is the smart thing.-

There's signs for the disabled, signs for ducks,-
Best ones are stickers, stuck on my truck.-

Like no one rides for free,-
Head, or gas, got weed.-

There's signs for every street,-
For the restaurants, where you eat.-

There's signs for the grocery stores, where you get gas,-
Road construction head, slow down, do not pass.-

There's sings for the rivers, for the lake,-
Signs for directions, on which hi-way you take.-

There's signs in the air, signs on the ground,-
Signs that are silent, some make sounds.-

There's signs I don't want to understand, ones I don't read,-
Some signs unimportant to me, agreed.-

Signs for every street, in the city, or county road,-
Even ones saying, heavy or wide load.-

So the next time, you get in your car, you see a sign,-
Don't pay attention, thinking you'll be fine.-

Like a school zone, or stop ahead,-
Because you didn't see the stop sign, how when it's red.-

Signs in the countertops, signs on glass,-
Consequences are yours, you can kiss my ass.-

THE END

Written by: Author and Poet
Robert E Rhines
January 14, 2018
Copyright applies

Sleep Walker

One wall, two wall, ceiling and door,-
Hearing footsteps running past, slapping the floor.-

Lights on after dusk, don't guide your day,-
Keeping your eyes closed, won't help you find your way.-

Concrete under carpet, you feel the solid ground,-
Ceiling overhead, your boxed in, starting to drown.-

One room, two room, three,-
Feeling yourself locked inside your dream.-

On the boundaries, at the edge, the sound of your name
calling,-
In the darkness, ahead or below, think it's past, as you
fall and keep falling.-

Frozen in time, on your way down,-
Your voice, trying to yell but can't make a sound.-

Trying to move, every muscle, bones froze,-
From the top of your head, to the tips of your toes.-

Your eyes think they can see, but they are not open, still
in bed,-
Sleep Walker your fall, your falling only in your head.-

It's like your brain can't translate,-
Somewhere your mind is, in an alternate state.-

Like your a sleep Walker, taking a stroll,
Wake up, stay in control.-

Inside, outside, door open, door close,-
Sleep Walker, is nothing you chose.-

All that's happening, not hearing a sound,-
Sleep Walker, your not falling, remember your on solid
ground.-

THE END

Written by; Author and Poet
Robert E Rhines
December 1, 2017
Copy rights apply

Snowflakes

I'm just sitting here, counting snowflakes, that fall,-
Heavy snowflakes, fall fast, can't count them all.-

Snowflakes don't fall in the same place,-
Watching them land on your face.-

I am so amazed,-
Snowflakes are so different, yet created the same.-

Snowflakes, some with patterns,-
Some drier, some more dampened.-

Like a raindrops splash, instantly freezes,-
Floating on a small drift of wind, winter breeze's.-

Falling here, falling there,-
Some land on water, and go no where.-

Landing on the roofs,
covering the ground,-
So light it's weight, falls and lands, without a sound.-

Yet it freezes, and it melts away,-
Until the next cold winters day.-

Blow the snow sideways, towards headlights,-
Blinds you, on bright.-

Like the fog, low beam is the way to go,-
Watch the lines, careful on the road.-

Care about life,-
Watch how you drive.-

Roads are slick, slick with ice,-
Specially when temperatures drop in the night.-

Careful of the black ice, you don't see,-
Turn your wheels the same way your sliding, take it
from me.-

Drive safe,-
Live another day.-

THE END

Written by: Author and Poet
Robert E Rhines
.January 25, 2018
Copyright applies

Songs about

You grab the guitar, I'll beat the drums,-
I'll start to sing, you start to hum.-

You pick the music, we'll keep the beat,-
We won't be rich, at least we'll eat.-

You strum the chords, let's keep the rhythm,-
It's all good, it's worth given.-

Songs about the future, songs about the past,-
Songs about life, and loves that didn't last.-

I'll play the harmonica, you play the sax,-
Songs about this, songs about that.-

We learn the tunes, we sing a long,
Songs about whiskey, songs about hitting the bong.-

We're not white trash, just blue collar,
Songs about the rich, songs about the ole mighty dollar.-

Songs about twin towers, songs about war,-
Songs about peace, we need more.-

Songs for you,
Songs for me,-

Songs for love,
Songs for world peace.-

THE END

Written by: Author and Poet
Robert E Rhines
January 7, 2018
Copyright applies

Soldier Man

Stranded in my mind,-
My thoughts find no mercy, the enemies not far behind.-

Eighteen years of age, barely a man,-
Joined the military, for a war, almost as senseless as
Vietnam.-

A seventeen year, senseless war,-
No reasons, the why's what ifs and what fores.-

Soldier Man

The sun's beating down, it's hot this day,-
Anxiety sets in hard, feeling these, my last words I'll say.-

Enemies lost, soldiers gone,-
But I can't help, but think about our song.-

Or the long walks,-
And the long talks.-

Soldier Man

I close my eyes, to get some relief,-
But it summons, way more grief.-

I'm hearing your voice, seeing your face,-
I just want to make it out, of this place.-

Our dogs barking, the kids playing,-
I'm hearing the words, your saying.-

Soldier Man

The days go on and on,-
The nights are even long.-

PTSD sets in,-
We're fighting an on going war, why don't it end.-

I try to stay fresh in thoughts, just to come home to you,-
But today turns out opposite, there is nothing else I
can do.-

Soldier Man

I try to stay optimistic,-
What comes next is realistic.-

First hit, second hit then the third,-
These my final words.-

You take care of yourself, and the dogs, raise our kids,-
There's no way I'll survive, these three hits.-

Times at hand,-
Soldier Man.-

An advocate and the Chaplin, bring you the news,-
I, like many others, fighting for freedom, a battle, I
thought I couldn't lose.-

I'm laying here, with my face, to the sky,-
A stranded soldier man,-
On foreign sand,-
One last tear in my eyes.-

If I could have, just one wish,-
Right here and now, one final kiss.-

Love your Soldier Man

THE END

Written by: Author and Poet
Robert E Rhines
March 5, 2018
Copyright applies

Spirit of the Mind

Just when I think, I've thought it all through, thought about
everything, hard,-
I say, I'll never let another, punch my card.-

In layman's terms,-
Where's all concerned.-

I've been tormented, lied to, and used,-
I will not, can not, let my heart be open for that same abuse.-

When it comes right down to it, I'm too soft at heart,-
And see, I think now, that Gods had his hand in it from the start.-

No matter, what I do, or what I say,-
It all comes back around, st the end of the day.-

At times, I've made it harder on myself, than it intended to be,-
Always a roll of the dice, a gamble, I jumped in with both feet.-
Ending with reflections, outcomes I feel but don't see.-

What's good for me, good for my heart, good for my soul,-
Happiness is what I seek, a dream of peace,-

It's not always about me, that's the reality,-
It's about the center, about balance, a common life, a common goal.-

Common, is not so common, now I see,-
But common does exist, it's within me.-

Life is a tale, a hard ride,-
On a journey here, come or step aside.-

There's nothing, no more, in me will I hide,-
Common is not so common, in body, or in the spirit of the mind.-

THE END

Written by: Author and Poet
Robert E Rhines
February 7, 2018

Standing Out

I've searched, year by year, and time goes by,-
Looked long, looked hard, and answers to why.-

I've let the things, I did go,-
I've agreed to, and said yes, and meant no.-

Standing up, standing out,-
No more being pushed or pulled about.-

Deep soul searching, I try,-
Questions with the answers, I had the whole time.-

Set your soul free,-
Sets your mind at ease,-

Dig deep down, find you,-
Look within find truth.-

Journeys, some short, some long,-
Without opinions, no reasons needed, be strong.-

Finding the center of you,-
Peace will come through.-

Though at times, it seems to fail,-
Other times, breathe and exhale.-

Standing out, differences in me,
You don't see,
I feel them now.-

THE END

Written by: Author and Poet
Robert E Rhines
February 3, 2018
Copyright applies

Stainless steel

I wear this cross around my neck,-
A symbol for the love I have for Jesus, I won't forget.-

Stainless steel,-
Beautiful.-

Handsomely made,-
Won't rust or fade.-

Shinny and bold,-
Stainless steel, not of gold.-

I wear it proud, for people to see,-
The love I have for Jesus, he died for me.-

I wear it with honor,-
Stainless steel, metal colour.-

There's others like it, but this one is mine,-
And I see it, you see it, stainless steel, look at it shine.-

A symbol, tried and true,-
Remember all, he not only died for me, he died for you.-

THE END

Written by: Author and Poet
Robert E Rhines
February 4, 2018
Copyright applies

# Still Fake

Cast out, the wrong, misleading and false temptations,-
Misunderstood signals, interrupted emotions.-

Hide behind, the mask your wearing,-
Walking softly, now won't stop my heart from tearing.-

Pack on the bondo, invisible behind make - up not on your face,-
With pain, you've pursued apologies, not a word, or a trace.-

Keep it real, can't stay strong, yourself will sustain,-
You'll always remember this mans name.-

Pat's on the back, laugh, your mouth returns that smile, how much more can it take,-
Your soul is ugly, sits dark, hide it deeper your still fake.-

From the feet, there's the toes,-
Throughout, way up to your nose.-

No beauty sits outside, or even within,-
Tasteless fashion, small accessories, about you where can I begin.-

One step ahead of your ex friend,-
I don't know where she starts, or you end.-

Looks about the mirror, what will it take,-
More endurance, drive, self worth and esteem, not enough your still fake.-

Hide in the shadows, stay in doors, til it's dark,-
Misjudged, underestimated, fire with no spark.-

Words fall from that hole under your nose,-
Your not all that, believe it, don't just stand there and pose .-

Matters now, nothing will it take,-
Inside and out, nobody's blind, cause your still fake.-

THE END

Written by: Author and Poet

R.E.R September 26,2017

uffering

I've seen some sadness on TV and in person,-
My life has been everything, but an excursion.-

To see suffering on TV, is out of my control,-
There's suffering right here in our backyards, that should
be the goal.-

People need to wake there asses up,-
We're the ones making it tough.-

Somehow it needs to be brought to the right attention,-
Not just tough on ourselves, third party at play, that's
all I'll mention.-

Honestly people need to understand what's really
going on,-
Anytime for real, we could be involved with our own
red dawn.-

There's enough suffering, if it's as important, it needs
direction then it's serious,-
American people have tolerated government officials,
they've deceived us, curious.-

How can we lay down for we've been suffering in
America now sometime,-

There wrong doings, they should all be charged for the crime.-

Suffering everyday in life, only shortens everyone's years,-
Its sickening, it's sad and hurtful my eyes fill with tears.-

Stand up for us, for your rights Americans,-
They're not asking, I'm telling it's more like, we listen to there demands.-

THE END

Written by: Author and Poet
Mr. R.E.Rhines
Sept 19, 2017

Take, Take, Take

Take, take, take, it's what takers do,-
They take from the innocent, from me, from you.-

Taking from others, is all they know,-
Take, take, take, from us no more.-

They take your pills, and leave you in pain,-
Selfish, for their own personal gain.-

Take, take, take, the shoes from your feet,-
They take the food, from your mouth, so they can eat.-

Take, take, take, money from your pocket,-
They take it from your safe, put away where you
locked it.-

Take, take, take the gas from your cars, from your truck,-
They take what's not nailed down, and say sorry about
your luck.-

Take, take, take, your self worth, your motivation,-
They take your lives, when you don't pay attention.-

Take, take, take, from you, from me,-
They take your happiness, all's left is there sorrow,
you see.-

Take, take, take, it's fun for them, it's there game,-
They leave you lost, broken, weakened without shame.-

I say,-
On this day.-
Take from me no more,-
For now I am under the protection of the Lord.-

THE END

Written by: Author and Poet
Robert E Rhines
Feb 9 2018
Copyrights applies

The Police

We wear this badge, we pack a gun,-
Remember, you beat me up, took my lunch money, yeah
I'm the one.-

There is no recourse, I'm the law,-
Above you and you, above you all.-

Talking on my cell phone, speeding when there's no
cause to,-
My radar gun, just got you.-

We're law enforcement,-
We'll take your drugs, your money and won't know
where it went.-

Also giving out tickets, it's what we do,-
Or we'll take you for a ride, cause we want to.-

No reason's, no more rights,-
When you see, flashing red and blue lights.-

Pull it on over, or we'll chase you down,-
We do what we want, were the law in this town.-

If you get on our bad side, or we don't like you,-
Better watch out for us, the boys in blue.-

A crime is committed, we don't care about the evidence,-
Whether your guilty or not is irrelevant.-

We're dirty, we don't care,-
Who says the law, has to be fare.-

We got you now locked up in jail,-
A few whispered words to the judge, no bail.-

If you have a weapon and don't comply,-
We'll shoot you, followed with a lie.-

We don't care about right or just,-
It's our way, not about trust.-

Give us more trouble than what we need,-
You'll end up in prison, never to be freed.-

Cause we're the police,-
Guns with badges own the streets.-

Run your mouth, get out of line,-
You'll wind up dead, it's a matter of time.-

The police have there own laws, you'll see,-
And you'll be a rebel, just like me.-

THE END

Written by: Author and Poet
Robert E Rhines
January 14, 2018
Copyright applies

The Story

We shake, we rattle and we roll,-
Spirits free, intertwined deep in the soul-.

Never a scout, but only for the minute,-
My life has more honor, now that your in it.-

And the roads we will embark,-
Together, and in this world we shall leave our mark.-

The thoughts of " I'll make you famous " come in view,-
Lifting each other, lifting me, lifting you.-

Now I won't make any promises, I can't own,-
But the connection has been made, out there to be
shown.-

Life is tricky, it's up's, it's down's,-
Weathering the storm, is not an option, stay solid, stay
sound.-

Longing to build for the long haul,-
I will give you my last breath, I gave you my all.-

Conversations are over here's, over there's,-
No guilt, of secrets all we share.-

End game is distant far from eminent,-
Not all paradise, not lies games only for the unfortunate

And it won't be all peaches and cream,-
We'll make this our story, our American dream.-

THE END

Written by: Author and Poet
Robert E Rhines
From me to you
Our first Christmas
December 4, 2017
Copyright applies

November 2017

There's Many

There's many different types, of people, doers and talker's,-
From the good souls to the evil stalkers.-

Doers jumping in, taking control,-
Talker's letting damage in life take its toll.-

There's many different types of people, movers and shakers,-
From lovers to heartbreakers.-

Movers working to get things done,-
Shakers coming up with excuses, you have one.-

There's many different types of people proud and or broken,-
From the carelessly loud, to the mousy and soft spoken.-

The proud walk tall, hi with no fear,-
Broken takes a nice long toke..... here.-

There's many different types of people some are boys, questionable ones, some are girls,-
It's a dog eat dog world.-

Boys we seem to think we have life beat,-
Til there's a girl involved and we're crying at there feet.-

Girls want to feel safe, a sense of security,-
A man not a boy with his childish immaturity.-

There's many different types of people, then there's you,
then there's me,-
Doesn't mean we have to stay lonely.-

You got life by the tail,-
Me I'll follow you, cause your on the right trail.-

THE END

Written by; Author and Poet
Robert E Rhines
End of November 2017

Til Then

Hands on the clock,-
Tic toc, tic toc.-
Water rising ever so slight,-
We stand on the dock, moons is among the stars bright.-

Temperatures hotter, contemplating thoughts of the first
date,-
Let thoughts stand down, the emotional kind, says
soulmate.-

Feeling like the touching kind,-
You've touched my heart, the word " Love"
not far behind.-

Seconds than minutes, turn hour into hour after hour,-
Just like the November rain's, turning to shower.-

Your hair is soaking wet,-
Radiant, glowing like the day we met.-

All the laughter, all the smiles,-
Made every moment of everyday, worthwhile.-

Twenty years, to the day,-
Looking at you, I love you in every way.-

Til then, remember tic toc, tic toc.-

You've been just as much " My Rock ".-

So with all these words,-
And every second, minute and hour, you are my self worth.-

Here's to your loyalty, here's to remaining friends,-
Keeping it real, enjoy our lives, year after year, mile after mile, til then.-

Til then, let the journey take us.........

THE END

Written by: Author and Poet
Robert E Rhines
Week one December 2017
Copyrights apply

Time never ends

Broken halos that shine,-
When I'm gone, I want mine.-

Strong wings, that help me fly,-
From here to there, throughout time.-

Helping others, helping you,-
My life, it's what I do.-

I'm back here, I've been here,-
How many times, it's unclear.-

Heaven exists, God awaits,-
Open arms, he stands at the gates.-

No pain, no tears,-
No drugs, no fears.-

A paradise, filled with love, filled with joy,-
Glorified through him, girls and boys.-

When I am gone, I'll be back, yet again,-
Broken halo, wings to fly, time never ends.-

Until we meet again, one day,-
For all of you, I will pray.-

Stay strong, as I will,-
Love for all, keep it real.-

In the end, you will see,-
Your own halo, your own wings, same as me.-

Over and over again, my friends,-
Time never ends.-

THE END

Written by: Author and Poet
Robert E Rhines
January 11, 2018
Copyright applies

The Devil

The Devil is knocking, don't look into his eyes,-
Broken promises, deceitful and full of lies.-
Does he have the power to die,-
The power to rise.-

The devil, only has power,-
In your weakest hour.-
Hides behind the lost, because he's a coward,-

The devil he manipulates,-
Our weaknesses to temp the fates,-
Full of jealousy, full of hate,-
Back away, now before darkness generates,-

The Devil, in his sick and twisted ways,-
Pain fills your life, during your weakest days,-
Cast him out, cast him out I say.-

The Devil, he offers up nothing good,-
Back away now, if you can, you should,-
I didn't have the strength, before now, but now I could.-

THE END

Written by : Author and Poet
Robert E Rhines
February 5, 2018
Copyright applies

The Voice

From the man, not a boy,-
Lines written, silent voice.-

Poetry tells a tale,-
From all walks of life, in prison, or in jail.-

Line after line,-
From no other voice now, but mine.-

Pick up the paper, pick up the pen,-
One after the other, let the story begin.-

Hard work, not easy you know,-
Verse after verse, the stories told.-

Written about life, written about truth,-
Written about all, written about youth.-

Over and over in my head,-
It's past, it's present, about the living, about the dead.-

Writing faster in my mind,-
My hand falls to sleep, falls behind.-

Keeping it real, staying in sight,-
It's all about life.-

Silence falls without sound,-
Except in my mind, no silence found.-

I write what I feel, I feel what I write,-
Sometimes in minutes, sometimes all night.-

My poetry is thoughts, silently spoken,-
By the grace of God, my pen is never broken.-

To all of you, these words are true,-
Understanding me, understanding you.-

From me to you, this small gift,-
For the ones lost, misplaced, or your spirits need a lift.-

Enjoy them, read them, let a smile warm your face,-
As mine is, while writing them, his voice, his Grace.-

THE END

Written by: Author and Poet
Robert E Rhines
January 28, 2018
Copyright applies

There's day's

There's day's good, day's bad,-
Day's happy, day's sad.-

And just days in between,-
some day's, I'm living the dream.-

There's day's sick, day's funny,-
Day's well, day's no money.-

And just day's, I lay and think,-
Some day's just plain stink.-

There's day's I walk, day's I run,-
Day's empty, day's fun.-

And just day's, I get by,-
Some day's, I don't know why.-

THE END

Written by: Author and Poet
Robert E Rhines
February 8, 2018

The Struggle

You try to run, you try to hide,-
To presumptuous in your convictions, it's about pride.-

Sometimes doing the right thing,-
Like following a dream.-

Is not the right thing at all,-
Stops you, sets you back, makes you fall.-

Dust off those knees,-
Really !!!! It's ok, please.-

Sit down write a list, of pros and cons,-
The pros being right, the cons being wrong.-

For every question, there's a correct answer,-
Life is an equation, your life matters.-

Repercussions for the wrong attempts,-
Consequences because you failed it.-

The struggle is real,-
You try to shrug it off, like no big deal.-

Sweep it clean, under the carpet,-
Or in the back of your mind, just to forget.-

We try to ride above the line,-
Pay our bills, and not fall behind.-

The struggle is real, no excuses,-
It's not always about the winners, it's about who loses.-

We are out here just trying to survive,-
We are out here, trying to stay alive,-
Out here with the killin, not wanting to die.-

Yeah the struggle is real, down and out,-
The struggle is real, here and now, no doubt.-

THE END

Written by: Author and Poet
Robert E Rhines
February 14, 2018

Tiptoe or Run

On a roll,-
Out of control.-

Without a mask I stand,-
What kind of man.-

Bills I let go, bills I pay,-
Words I hold within, words I say.-

Same old same,-
Everyday changes, but your name.-

Hours come, hours go,-
Accomplishments, hard work and it shows.-

Day end, nights come,-
Time is never enough.-

Reach out, reach in,-
The depth of your soul, awaits begin.-

The darkness blinds you, blinds me,-
Oh Lord, help us see.-

See what's ahead, not what's behind,-
Even on the bad days, let me shine.-

Not all joy, not all pain remember, and forget,-
Good days, bad days money earned, money spent.-

Tiptoe or Run,-
Tests daily, tests passed, tests one by one.-

On a roll,-
Next test, here we go.-

Take it fast, end it slow,-
Some we'll pass, some we won't.-

Sometimes were not meant to know the answers,-
Sometimes our trials end with disasters.-

Roll on, roll on,-
Live for today, tomorrow's, tomorrow your gone.-

THE END

Together

Together, life is supposed to be a grand design,-
What is yours, what is mine.-

Together, we laugh, drink, and party without care,-
The music we hear, to the songs we share.-

Together, strong, but not above the outside world,-
I'm your boy, your my girl.-

Together, as others come, as others go,-
Out lasting me, outlasting? You'll never know.-

Together, we brought ourselves, at the bar,
Faded out, gone! Not to far.-

Together, happiness did sit within you, within me,-
Now there's nothing I feel for you, how you don't see.-

Together, I'd see a hint of a smile,-
Nice I thought, deceiving all the while.-

Together, there is no other way, no! Not a chance,-
Split, you went your way, continuing my own dance.-

Together, never, really just a bad taste,-
I gave you time, I got returned, a slap in the face.-

THE END

Written by: Author and Poet
R.E.Rhines Sept. 29,2017

Troubled Past

A girl born into the wild, the bush, jungle as it's called,-
Things she's seen, had to do, most would be appalled.-

Having no real childhood, and growing up before her time,-
Not being able to be a child, itself should be a crime.-

Prostitution is known throughout the jungle within many camps,-
It's the only way to get cash on hand for drugs, alcohol most of em only get food stamps .-

The jungle is a city of its own,-
Hands on experience, instead of being shown.-

From camp to camp girls being sold for what's in need,-
Could be for cash, dope, or alcohol, tobacco even weed.-

She'll grow up twenty five years in this place,-
After all is vacant within, keeps a smile on her face.-

After having four children of her own,-
She returns to the beginning, where her heart is, home.-

Custody of the kids are placed maybe on the Father's or others,-
Why or how could she give up being a mother.-

Bouncing man to man in search to fill the void in her heart,-
There drug addicts and homeless, filthy and doomed from the start.-

Its difficult for her to only be with one,-
As soon as it's serious, she'll cut and run.-

A young woman with a troubled past,-
Damaged significantly, relations cant last.-

If there is ever to be a future, regular life she could live,-
Stop helping others, she always ready to give.-

No better livelihood than the rest,-
Doing for others, putting herself in a mess.-

Troubled by thirty four years of pain,-
Always there, never forget, locked in her brain .-

Parents adapt the children in horror, living this way,-
Need to be dealt with swiftly, max punishment I'd say.-

THE END

Written by author and poet Mr R.E.R
For Tara Rodrieks
September 17,2017

Two Things

There's only two things, certain in life,-
That's living or you die.-

Just like a soldier's, last letter to a wife, he's fallen,-
Feeling the wetness of the tears,-
Crying sounds in your ears,-
Gun fire ringing and in the distance, children bawlin.-

There's only two things, certain in life,-
Single as in alone, or married, man and wife.-

Just like a soldier's, country truc,
As is the love of a woman, like you.-

There's things we handle alone,-
But we're not.-
Together we built this home,-
It's what we got.-

There's only two things certain in life,-
Doing wrong, doing right.-

Like a soldier, fighting for, not country but cause,-
In the jurisdiction of foreign laws,-

Keeping his mind back home, on the family he loves,-

Elsewhere when there is war to be fought,-

Believing in you Lord, save us all, walking in your steps, heaven above,-

A flying half staff flag, twenty one gun shots,-

THE END

Written by: Author and Poet
Robert E Rhines
He is love, he is life
December 5, 2017

Two X girl

Welcome, to my world,-
Two X girl.-

Don't just sit on that bum,-
Get some.-

Two X butt,-
So what .-

It's not all about, the "look",-
Or if you can clean, or cook.-

It's not about the size of your thighs,-
Or that you like, burgers and fries.-

Welcome to my world,-
Two X girl.-

Don't just call, when your alone,-
Call anytime I have a phone.-

D's work, fine by me,-
Double D's.-

It's not all about the outside, what's within,-
You got the number, you can call again.-

Its not about the size of your body,-
Just because your not skinny, or know karate.-

Two X girl,-
You rock my world.-

If I had to rate you, on a scale, your a one,-
And add a zero after it, done.-

I'm not a judge, I don't rate,-
My two X girl, my friend, my date.-

So your a ten,-
My Two X friend.-

THE END

Written by: Author and Poet
Robert E Rhines
January 24, 2018

Unforseen Peace

As I walk as far as the eyes can see, I walk this beach,-
I take in the deepest breaths, I inhale your peace.-

With the light drizzles of rain, with the winds in my face,-
I am one with you oh Lord, I am one in your grace.-

Take me oh Lord, in your arms,-
Embrace me, hold me let life›s darkness bring unto me,
no harm›s.-

As I walk, you are with me, your spirit never leaves,-
The sounds of the winds, the sounds of the seas.-

I am one, in your love, I am one in this place,-
Let your Love's warmth, warm my face.-

I have walked, broken roads,-
I have lived in selflessness, I have never walked alone.-

For you are my shepherd, you are all things of peace,-
Though you are with me, only in spirit, I am not alone
on this beach.-

THE END

Written by: Author and Poet
Robert E Rhines
February 11, 2018
Copyright applies

Remember when

Remember when....

I was little, first steps taken, just learning to walk,-
Da da my first word spoken, learning to talk.-

Alot of mis-steps, I would stumble,-
You'd laugh, a voice of joy, your voice kind, very humble.-

Bumps and bruises, from all the falls,-
You'd cry, tears and all.-

I'd fall, we both cried,- you'd wipe those tears, from my
eyes.-

You'd get me to giggle, get me to laugh,-
Looking back now, time went so fast.-

Remember when......

You were there for me, I needed your help,-
You'd always think of me first, before anything else.-

Playing with my trucks in the front yard,-
I'd get into trouble, you'd spank me hard.-

I'd look at you, with my eyes of blue,-
Tears welling in my eyes,-

It hurt me, also hurt you,-
And now I understand why.-

Love the ultimate bond,-
Love you always, Dad, love your son.-

THE END

Written by: Author and Poet
Robert E Rhines
February 5, 2018
Copyright applies

Copyright applies

Ungrateful

Could be a stranger, could be a friend,-
You've done what you could, they're ungrateful in the end.-

Someone close, someone afar,-
You find out how ungrateful they really are.-

Money they owe, money they borrow,-
One excuse after the next, every word full of sorrow.-

A place to stay, a place to live,-
Ungrateful on their part, the more you give.-

Maybe clothing, or an inanimate object,-
You loaned them your car, now it's wrecked.-

Ungrateful, sorry they say,-
Then they want to borrow something else from you, the very next day.-

Just so full, of excuse,-
Ungrateful to the point, what's the use.-

If they can't be grateful, for the things you do,-
You continue to help the ungrateful, then the blame falls on you.-

There's the ungrateful,-
And theirs the grateful.-
God I am grateful, and I am thankful.-

For you.... your guidance helps me along my way, grateful
for you being in my life each and every day.-

THE END

Written by: Author and Poet
Robert E Rhines
February 9, 2018
Copyright applies

e Fit

Crisp early morning, up before the dawn, beautiful day,-
Tennessee to Texas, back home, on your way.-

Fantastic, fulfilled weekend,-
Amazing time, my friend.-

Tears well up, in our eyes,-
See you later, I'm no good at goodbyes -

Stopped by the station, tank is all filled,-
Crying like babies, like our best friend's just been killed.-

Silly and utterly goofy, with emotions,-
Like a roller coaster ride, on the waves of the ocean.-

Laying close, side by side,-
Everything's out in the open, secrets we won't hide.-

Our bodies entangled, lying silent, as our mouths talk,-
For hours about anything, everything, we can't stop.-

Wee hours begin, yet another,-
The beds a mess, you stole all the covers.-

We're off on something few, far and between,-
Nervous as hell, even after the breaking of the ice, you
know what i mean.-

Birth signs GEMINI on Leo,-
From here, where do we go.-

You back to Texas, I'll stay in Tennessee,-
Lonely, shame on you, lonely me.-

It's been great, it's been fun,-
You get in your SUV, off on the run.-

It's only temporary, we will see,-
No doubt, I fit you, you fit me.-

We fit together like a hand in a glove,-
Life ..... live.....love.....

THE END

Written by: Author and Poet
Robert E Rhines
December 11, 2017

e lose

Stomp, stomp the vibration underfoot,-
Ten thousand, top cover to boot.-

Merit badges to strips on the arm,-
Listen, listen closely you've been warned.-

We do back up, but we won't back down,-
Commin in hot, radio spills, as we hit the ground.-

Tat, tat gunfire, explosions fill my ears,-
Heartbeats, deep breaths, hold back the fears.-

Dusk to dawn,-
The gunfire goes on.-

Sense's guessing, on unfamiliar sounds,-
Ringing in your ears, like water, your start to drown.-

Endless minutes, so many thoughts, come to mind,-
As I lay here, am I left behind.-

Like a suspension in time, fear just came to life,-
Now, will you make it thru this night.-

The fight goes on, if we, if we choose,-
It's when we give up, we lose.-

THE END

Written by :Author and Poet
Robert E Rhines
January 3, 2018

We pass by

News clips of sadness,-
Chaos in the streets, much violence, complete madness.-

Bits of tears, bits of pain, that never takes a holiday,-
Every day continues, it never ends, and never goes away.-

From all the gun shots,-
Cars being stolen, people being robbed.-

And the terror that grows in our nation,-
The end, our book is Revelation.-

We see it getting worse, tears never dry,-
Only we can stop it, working together, we gotta try.-

The worst, when I hear about the children, it's so sad,-
It makes me sick, to my stomach, drives the calm in
me mad.-

We pass by,-
Cover the sounds in our ears, the sights in our eye.-

Wars in foreign lands,-
When our own home grounds, in itself out of hand.-

Veterans homeless, in the streets,-
With no place to sleep, no food to eat.-

The world is going, more sideways,-
And the evils growing more, in the coming days.-

It's time we've stopped, take a long hard look around,-
How can you get on with your lives, like your def, like
your blind, to what's going down.-

We pass by,-
Not paying attention, the world dies.-

THE END

Written by: Author and Poet
Robert E Rhines
February 13, 2018
Copyright applies

Words

Words, between a man and a woman, from a woman to
a man,-
Shouldn't be short, or out of hand.-

Words, to raise encouragement,-
From the heart, not the mouth of disappointment.-

Words, meant not to tear down, meant to lift,-
From me to you, a respectful gift.-

Words of accomplishments,-
From the soul, acknowledgements.

Words wrongfully misused, wrongfully mistaken,-
From one heart, or the other is breaking.-

Words transformed in our minds, before saying,-
On our knees, hands are praying.-

Words of wisdom, words of mine,-
From your heart, from my heart, always kind.-

Words, solum, words to teach,-
From the depths, within us they reach.-

Words of love, to God we praise,-
From strangers on the streets, to our children we raise.-

Words, we are blessed, simplicity,-
From me to you, and everyone else in between.-

THE END

Written by: Author and Poet
Robert E Rhines
January 27, 2018
Copyright applies

You and God

Thank you God, for who I am,-
But you know, I am a better man.-

Working on me, one day at a time,-
Everything in life, falling in line.-

You see to that, believing is a test,-
I must have passed, I'm blessed.-

Thank you God, for the way you let me see,-
Working on the world, working on all, working on me.-

You see to that, all my needs are met,-
Hard times came and went.-

Thank you God, for all that I hear,-
Working on happiness in some, others put in fear.-

You see to that, all cares,-
Life is good, though sometimes not fare.-

Thank you God, for the ability to change,-
Walking in the light, instead of the dark, strange.-

You see to that, I'm here to stay,-
And I know now, with your love, I am saved.-

Thank you God, for your love,-
Way beyond the heavens above.-

You see to that, my heart's filled,-
And I help others, faith in you, love rebuilds.-

Thank you God, for who I am today,-
Reaching others, teaching others your way.-

You see to that, through you, our faith,-
We all can be changed, be saved.-

THE END

Written by: Author and Poet
Robert E Rhines
January 21, 2018
Copyright applies

You Can't

Make up your mind,-
Take your time.-

Give up your answer,-
Let fall, all the disaster.-

From the strong, and the weak,-
From the mild, and the meek.-

Earth being your beginning, the lay over place,-
Excepting the terror, letting it rein, before we except
your grace.-

Where are you going?, not about distance, by how far,-
Staying behind, or out there somewhere, amongst the
stars.-

You can't get there, by bus, or a plane,-
It's about receiving, his love, praising his name.-

You can't get there, by thumbing a ride,-
Or taking your car, out for a drive.-

You can't get there, by boat, by ship,-
Ask him into your heart, let the words pass, only your
lips.-

You can't get there, by land, by air or Sea,-
Let him save you, as he saved me.-

You can't get there, by mere man, rockets or machine,-
Receive him, why not? he's already died for the sin, it's
real not a dream.-

You can't get there, by any other means,-
Accept him, receive him, pray on your knees.-

He holds out, he waits for you,-
In us he believes, should we not believe in him too.-

He counts the days, he waits to return,-
Through him only, your saved, you'll learn.-

He's patient, he's understanding, he's kind,-
I walk on a personal journey with God, like he's a friend
of mine.

THE END

Written by: Author and Poet
Robert E Rhines
January 16, 2018
Copyright applies

You can't outwit God

Stop and think about, the things, some people have said,-
There is no God, God is dead.-

Those people inadvertently don't understand,-
The sacrifice of one Father, the consequences to a son,
the death of a man.-

It's not just the death of a man, but the death of our
Lord,-
A death for some, supposed to even a score.-

A score, to help save us all,-
If you can't understand the truth, you'll never understand
at all.-

You can't outwit God,-
For he is thy staff, he is thy rod.-

He is thy tears, he is thy strength,-
He is all, many things.-

God sees it all, knows it before it's said,-
God is alive in us all, God is not dead.-

There's some you can get over on,-
But you can't outwit God.-

And you think you know it all,-
You know nothing, like the rest that rebuke him, you to
shall fall.-

Except it, love him, live it,-
For in the end, you lose, God will win, God will outwit.-

THE END

Written by: Author and Poet
Robert E Rhines
February 13, 2018
Copyright applies

Printed in the United States
By Bookmasters